The Dumbing of Canadian Democracy

The Fall of Responsible Government

Peter Boer

© 2014 by Folklore Publishing
First printed in 2014 10 9 8 7 6 5 4 3 2 1
Printed in China

All rights reserved. No part of this work covered by the copyrights hereon may be reproduced or used in any form or by any means—graphic, electronic or mechanical—without the prior written permission of the publisher, except for reviewers, who may quote brief passages. Any request for photocopying, recording, taping or storage on information retrieval systems of any part of this work shall be directed in writing to the publisher.

The Publisher: Folklore Publishing

Website: www.folklorepublishing.com

Library and Archives Canada Cataloguing in Publication

Boer, Peter, 1977–, author
    The dumbing of Canadian democracy: the fall of responsible government / Peter Boer.

Includes bibliographical references.

ISBN 978-1-926677-92-7 (pbk.)

1. Political corruption—Canada. 2. Canada—Politics and government—2006–. I. Title.

FC643.S3B64 2014   971.07'3   C2014-904850-5

Project Director: Faye Boer
Project Editor: Nicholle Carrière
Cover Image: © JuanDarien / Thinkstock; *back cover:* background © JuanDarien / Thinkstock; bird © Marija_piliponyte / Thinkstock

Produced with the assistance of the Government of Alberta, Alberta Media Fund.

We acknowledge the financial support of the Government of Canada through the Canada Book Fund (CBF) for our publishing activities.

 Canadian Heritage   Patrimoine canadien

PC: 27

Dedication

For my uncle,
Louis John Dziedzic
March 13, 1938–July 22, 2014

Acknowledgements

Thanks, as always, go first and foremost to my mother, Faye, for her continued support of my work. None of this work would be possible without the love and support of my wife Kathy and my son Christopher—thank you for everything. And to all the journalists out there who work too hard and are paid too little to hold those in public office to account—you are making a difference.

Contents

Foreword by Brent Rathgeber 7

Introduction 12

Chapter 1: Chuck Cadman Affair 19

Chapter 2: In-and-Out Scandal 42

Chapter 3: Afghan Detainee Affair 56

Chapter 4: Maxime Bernier Affair. 83

Chapter 5: 2008 Prorogation of Parliament 103

Chapter 6: F-35 Purchase Scandal 124

Chapter 7: Guergis-Jaffer Scandal. 154

Chapter 8: Robocalls Scandal. 193

Chapter 9: Omnibus Bills 214

Chapter 10: Senate Expense Scandal 223

Conclusion 252

Bibliography 258

Foreword

By Brent Rathgeber

– Member of Parliament for Edmonton-St. Albert;
Author of *Irresponsible Government: The Decline of
Parliamentary Democracy in Canada*

Responsible Government is the constitutional convention that mandates that the elected Parliament is supreme and the appointed executive cabinet is responsible and accountable to it. For a government to govern, it must at all times enjoy the confidence of Parliament or a provincial legislature. Responsible Government is maintained when a government that has lost the confidence of the elected assembly must either resign or face the electorate.

Accordingly, Parliament is designed as a tripwire or important check and balance on executive power.

Tripwires are placed strategically and purposely into any functioning system. In the electrical sense, a fuse is tripped to prevent a malfunctioning appliance from causing a power surge and a fire. In the Organizational Behaviour context, tripwires or checks and balances exist to assure that decisions made are correctly and that risks for misappropriations are minimized.

In the democratic context, checks and balances similarly exist to assure that decisions are vetted and validated and that tax dollars are accounted for. Parliament is theoretically the ultimate check in the democratic process. The Cabinet must maintain Parliament's confidence, seek its approval to spend monies and submit legislation to it for vetting and approval.

In the real world, everybody is accountable to somebody. A file clerk reports to a supervisor, who reports to a manager, who answers to a director, who reports to a vice president, who answers to a president, who answers to a Board of Directors, which is accountable to the stockholders.

Each level of accountability is a deliberate attempt to minimize risk and assure quality control.

In the context of Canadian democracy, the important tripwire of cabinet accountability to Parliament, whose Members are answerable to their constituents began to break down a half century ago. As the Canadian population grew and as government got into the business of universal social programs, by necessity, government grew.

As government grew, there was a corresponding increase in the size of the federal cabinets. Soon Prime Ministers found it difficult to chair focused meetings with thirty or more ministers in the room so they began to break cabinet up into more functionally sized units. Cabinet committees such as the Treasury Board, and Planning and Priorities became the power brokers. With bureaucrats and political staffers becoming more important in providing the expertise to these cabinet committees, it was decided to centralize said mandarins in the Privy Council Office, and eventually, the Prime Minister's Office.

Within fifty years, Parliamentary Supremacy had been replaced, first by Executive Government (Cabinet) and more recently by an unhealthy consolidation of power inside the Office of the Prime Minister. This trend would not nearly be so destructive if the other institutions provided checks and balances to executive power, but they do not, and within the confines of current power dynamics, they cannot.

Promotion within the system depends on accumulated political capital. Backbenchers desire to be mid- and eventually front-benchers. Similarly, upwardly mobile bureaucrats are more likely to be promoted through sycophancy than for speaking truth to power.

The consequences of centralized power and non-functioning or non-existent tripwires should be obvious.

It is obvious to some, but sadly, it is obscure to those who wield power without the meaningful checks and balances.

Budget bills receive inadequate scrutiny; deficit financing becomes the norm, leading a wealthy country to be burdened by in excess of $650 billion in national debt. Crime bills are not properly vetted, and many of them are subsequently deemed unconstitutional and non-Charter compliant by the courts. Scientists are muzzled, environmental legislation is repealed and replaced by ill-thought-out regulatory schemes, and in the process, a country's black-eyed reputation excludes it from responsible resource development and marketing.

With the tripwires systemically removed and ineffective checks and balances in place, ethical lapses are inevitable and will go undetected until discovered by external agencies such as the media or legal authorities.

Only an absence of checks and balances can explain how a twenty-two-year-old political staffer and election volunteer can get wrapped up in a scheme to direct hundreds of non-Conservative supporters to nonexistent polling stations on Election Day. Michael Sona has been sentenced to nine months in jail; the judge stated others were involved. How could nobody second guess such a foolhardy, illegal, unethical and ultimately unsuccessful attempt at voter suppression?

Only in a procurement that is allowed to proceed on the basis of a sole-sourced "competition" can a plane be chosen in advance and then the specifications developed to rationalize and justify that choice, and then millions of dollars spent in research and prototype development, while Canadian taxpayers are nowhere near owning any actual fighter jets.

But the apex of a system of deficient checks and balances is highlighted by the Duffy-Wright Debacle, where a senator falsely claimed $90,000 in housing expenses and then the prime minister's chief of staff gifted the same to that sitting legislator in exchange for his cooperation in sanitizing an audit report regarding those very expenses.

A minimum of a "few" or perhaps as many as a dozen highly placed denizens of the Prime Minister's inner circle knew about some aspect of the nefarious plot and either agreed it was a good scheme or were powerless to prevent it. Ethical boundaries were breached and laws likely broken. This is the inevitable outcome of a system operating in the absence of quality control. This is the sad culmination of an operating system where nobody questions another's judgement, and sycophancy is preferred over constructive criticism. Scandal is the inevitable product of non-functioning checks and balances.

Scandal may be the apex of centralized power operating absent of checks and balances but waste, inefficiency and disrespect for taxpayers are its lesser by-products. All represent a difference in degree of unaccountable, centralized decision making. A government that refuses to allow itself to be held to account becomes by definition unaccountable.

The Harper Conservative Government is hardly the first Canadian administration to be plagued by multiple scandals, waste and mismanagement. The Harperites replaced a Liberal Government, whose infamy includes the Sponsorship Scandal, where $100 million was diverted to Liberal-friendly advertising agencies in Québec for little to no work, and the HRDC Debacle, where $1 billion in employment programs could neither be traced nor accounted for. The Chretien/Martin Liberals replaced the Mulroney government, which in its later years became almost synonymous with scandal and ethical lapses.

However, the incidents of waste, mismanagement and gross misjudgement are becoming more frequent. Eventually, so-called isolated incidents coagulate and metastasize into a cancer of untrustworthiness. The dysfunction, however, is systemic not personal. Just as changing governments in 2006 did nothing to minimize waste, mismanagement and disappointment, changing the personalities again, without changes to the system, will do little to provide effective oversight and accountability.

Former journalist Peter Boer clearly points out and describes the unavoidable effects of centralized power operating in the absence of effective oversight. Taxpayers concerned about wasteful appropriations and non-merit awarded contracts may be alarmed to read his analysis. Similarly, ethicists and promoters of the law will be shocked to learn of the extent and occasional sophistication of some of the plots and schemes of inside players, who prefer to operate without accountability. All Canadians, interested in promoting peace, order and good and responsible government would do well by studying the effect and consequences of not restoring accountability to Canadian democracy. Boer's analysis is clear, well researched and devastating.

We need to reinstall effective checks and balances to assure quality control. A government accountable to an elected Parliament, whose members prefer loyalty to their constituents over their party, will provide the antidote to centralized authority, accountable to no one other than itself.

Introduction

SCANDAL, I BELIEVE, is inevitable when power is involved. I don't think there has been a government in Canadian history in which someone did not act improperly at one point or another. But in the case of Stephen Harper's Conservative government, the scandal seems to be more pointed simply because of the wave of public support that swept Harper and the Conservatives to a minority government in 2006. It was scandal that felled Paul Martin's Liberals when the Auditor General laid clear the scope and depth of the sponsorship scandal, the woeful program to heighten the government's profile in Québec after the 1995 sovereignty referendum. While perhaps a good idea when it was conceived, the fact that little or no work was done, coupled with the fact that Liberal-friendly ad agencies that received contracts funnelled some of that money back into the Québec wing of the Liberal Party, was as sensational a scandal as Canada had endured in recent memory. Paul Martin might very well have been "mad as hell," but Canadians were even angrier and decided to give the Stephen Harper Conservatives a shot at government.

The Harper government had hammered the Liberals with the Auditor General's findings on the sponsorship scandal, and when they formed the government, the Conservatives tried to portray themselves as the squeaky clean, accountable alternative to the Liberals, even going so far as to pass their Accountability Act to try to mitigate future problems such as the sponsorship scandal. However, the number of scandals and questionable acts that the Conservatives have been involved in suggests that they have failed in their efforts to govern from a moral higher ground.

INTRODUCTION

All ten scandals and questionable actions within this book are recent in memory, encompassing a period of approximately eight years. In fact, the genesis of one scandal, in the case of the late Chuck Cadman, dates back to the Conservatives' days as the official opposition to Paul Martin's Liberals. Regardless of what party is in power, people are still capable of behaving poorly, sometimes criminally. Which way on the political spectrum they lean doesn't make any one party more benevolent or morally rigorous than another. Put any group of individuals in power, and scandal of some kind is inevitable.

Consider that this book doesn't even cover all the questionable actions of the Conservative government. Missing owing to space constraints is the tale of Bev Oda, the large-spending former Conservative and cabinet member. Her story was particularly egregious for the Conservatives, given their natural tendency to portray themselves as the best possible keeper of the public purse. During her time as minister, Oda travelled to the 2005 Juno Awards and incurred almost $5500 in limousine rides, only $2200 of which she repaid. In 2011, when she attended a conference on immunizing poor children, she decided against staying at the pre-arranged hotel and instead stayed at a hotel that charged $665 per night for three nights. It was during this stay that she ordered the infamous $16 glass of orange juice, but she also rode around in a limousine and was fined $250 for smoking in a non-smoking room. Oda was also taken to task for telling her staff to change a signed Canadian International Development Agency (CIDA) memo by hand. The result of the change was that a funding recommendation for one group did not proceed. An ensuing investigation led to a ruling by the Speaker of the House that Oda should be investigated further, but before that could take place, the Conservatives were brought down over the finding of contempt of Parliament for their failure to turn over documents requested by the House of Commons. Yet the Conservatives emerged from that election with a majority government.

Bev Oda is not the only member of Parliament to behave badly. Consider the case of Maxime Bernier, a former rising star within the Conservative Party because he was one of their only Québec MPs. Bernier started dating Julie Couillard, who had past connections with organized biker gangs in Québec. Bernier even went so far as to leave confidential documents at Couillard's home for a period of five weeks. The fallout cost him his cabinet position as Minister of Foreign Affairs. Bernier has only recently found his way back to a cabinet post.

There was also the case of former MP Helena Guergis and her husband, former MP Rahim Jaffer, who helped make the expression "busty hookers" an entry in Canadian political history. Guergis first made headlines for throwing a temper tantrum at the airport in Charlottetown, but went on to make more when one of Guergis' assistants started sending letters to the editors of different local newspapers heaping praise on the MP. The scandal reached its height when Harper punted her from caucus and called in the RCMP amid rumours that Guergis and her husband were spending time with less-than-reputable characters and might even be involved with prostitutes, cocaine and fraud. Guergis lost her seat in the 2011 election and has since spent her time studying law and trying to sue the Conservative Party.

INTRODUCTION 15

Then there were the Senators. Not the Ottawa NHL team, but the trio of Conservative senators—plus Liberal Mac Harb—who created a sensation in Ottawa with their allegedly fraudulent expense claims. Pamela Wallin and Mike Duffy left the Conservative caucus and were suspended from the Senate over trying to claim ineligible expenses. Duffy's case was considered the most sensational because a member of Harper's own staff helped him pay back the $90,000 he improperly claimed. Included, too, was Patrick Brazeau, who not only got himself charged by the RCMP over his expenses, but was also arrested twice at his own home under unfortunate circumstances.

Other, larger scandals have had their roots in the government and party as a whole. The In-and-Out scandal, which was so boring that no one really paid much attention to it as a true scandal, saw the Conservatives trying to play fast and loose with campaign finance law in their advertising during the 2006 election. The Conservatives were caught moving money between their national campaign and local campaigns in an attempt to get around campaign spending limits. It ended with the Conservatives paying back approximately $230,000.

The Afghan detainee scandal saw the Conservative government on the defensive over allegations during the war in Afghanistan. Detainees taken into custody by Canadian soldiers and handed over to Afghan custody were subjected to abuse and torture, a violation of the Geneva Convention. The Conservatives kept secret one instance in which transfers were suspended owing to the suspicion of abuse. Opposition requests for more information led to a precedent-setting ruling by the Speaker of the House asserting the supremacy of Parliament over the government.

Then the Conservatives tried to buy some new airplanes for the military, announcing that they would spend $16 billion ($9 billion to buy, $7 billion to maintain) on an unproven fighter jet, the F-35. This despite a series of reports that revealed Canada would have to pay a lot more than $7 billion to maintain the fighters for their expected lifespan. The controversy over the purchase led to the government publicly backing away from its intention to pursue the sole-source contract. As of the writing of this book, no decision has been made as to whether or not the Conservative government will go ahead with the purchase.

Then there was the prorogation of Parliament in 2008. Remember that? When the Conservatives seemed to completely misjudge the extent of the coming recession and tried, instead of stimulating the economy, to eliminate political funding for its opposition parties? The Conservatives were faced with a full-scale revolt in the House of Commons, and the spectre of Canada being led by a Liberal-NDP coalition reared its head. Harper was eventually granted his prorogation, but not before castigating the Liberals and the NDP for consorting with the Bloc Québécois, all the while forgetting about the times that the Conservatives had done so.

There was also the robocalls scandal, in which it appeared at first that there was a large, concerted effort to suppress votes across the country. The robocalls were automated telephone calls telling voters their polling stations had been moved when, in fact, that was not the case. There were also early allegations of deliberately rude phone calls that seemed to be from Liberals, as if they were trying to offend voters enough to prevent them from voting, but little evidence of that was ever found.

Although the evidence later pointed to a more isolated conspiracy in the riding of Guelph, Ontario, it was telling how many people thought the Conservatives were responsible for a larger conspiracy. Michael Sona, a campaign worker, was later found guilty for his role in the scandal.

And, as mentioned earlier, there was Chuck Cadman, who the Conservatives allegedly tried to sway to vote in their favour with promises of an enormous life insurance policy for a man who was dying of cancer. It was Cadman whose vote as an Independent member of the House of Commons saved the Liberals from falling on a confidence vote over their 2005 budget. The ensuing scandal led to a lawsuit against the Liberal Party, which was eventually settled out of court.

A look at the bibliography will show that the bulk of the sources for this book came from the *National Post*. That decision was deliberate. It's a good paper, but the pointed use of their stories is more an exercise in political balance. The *Post* is unabashedly supportive of the Conservatives, so using its stories and commentaries in my research is a defence of sorts against any allegations that I relied on "the liberal media."

The one constant in many of these scandals isn't just the Conservatives or members of the government behaving badly, but also how poorly Stephen Harper and the Conservatives treat other people. When faced with criticism or challenged over their positions, Harper and the Conservatives prefer to lash out, to try to smear the reputations of people attempting to point out their errors. Whether he is intimating that critics are lying, claiming that the opposition's questions about detainee abuse are proof that the opposition supports the Taliban or kicking one of his own MPs to the curb over salacious, unsubstantiated accusations, it seems clear that Harper has little regard for the people around him. It appears that people, in Harper's view, are expendable casualties of him staying in power. Perhaps it's naïve of me, but I expect better of the leader of our country.

This book is testimony to the fact that such expectations are likely unrealistic.

CHAPTER ONE

Chuck Cadman Affair

It was one of the most riveting political dramas to play itself out on the Canadian parliamentary stage, and though Stephen Harper was not yet in government, it would come to represent one of the first scandals that would befall his government once he did become prime minister.

It was the spring of 2005, and Prime Minster Paul Martin was fighting to pass a budget in the face of a majority opposition. He had secured, after much negotiating, a deal with the NDP that would see the opposition party support the Liberals in passing the budget, but it had come at a cost. Specifically, NDP leader Jack Layton had asked the Liberals to remove $4.6 billion in corporate tax cuts from the proposed budget. In its place, the NDP wanted to see a boost in social spending, including the addition of $1.5 billion for training programs and university tuition assistance, $1.6 billion for low-income housing, $900 million for environmental measures and another $500 million in foreign aid.

The Conservatives, led by Stephen Harper, promptly announced that they would defeat the Liberal government "at the earliest possible opportunity."

Harper's threat had a significant amount of weight to it at the time. The Conservatives held 99 seats in the

House of Commons, and the Bloc Québécois, who also pledged to defeat the budget deal, held 54 seats, for 153 seats combined. The NDP had won 19 seats in the last election and the Liberals 135 seats, but the Liberals now sat with fewer than that number—Labrador member of Parliament Lawrence O'Brien had died in December 2004 of cancer, and a by-election to fill his seat was not scheduled until May 24, 2005. Two members of the Liberal Party were also now sitting as Independents in the House of Commons: Carolyn Parrish (Mississauga-Erindale) and David Kilgour (Edmonton-Millwoods-Beaumont). Parrish had been expelled from the Liberal caucus in November 2004 after a *This Hour Has 22 Minutes* sketch showed her stomping on and pretending to perform voodoo on a doll representing then-U.S. President George W. Bush. David Kilgour, a former Conservative MP who left the Tory caucus over the GST, had departed from the Liberal caucus in April 2005 over the ongoing sponsorship scandal and Canada's lack of action in the conflict in Darfur.

There was one more Independent MP in the House, but he was different from Kilgour and Parrish in that he hadn't left a party to sit as an Independent—he had been elected as an Independent. He was also different from every other MP in the House of Commons because he took his seat typically clad in jeans instead of a more formal suit and tie. He wore his hair long and in a ponytail. His name was Chuck Cadman, and he had represented the riding of Surrey North since 1997.

He hadn't always sat as an Independent. In fact, Cadman had first been elected as a member of the Reform Party, which had, over time, morphed first into the Canadian Alliance and then into the present-day

Conservative Party. Before that, he had played a lot of guitar, even touring at one point for a band called The Fringe and playing for The Guess Who on CBC Television. He had also worked as a camera technician.

But a personal tragedy had pushed Cadman into the public eye, which in turn led him to Ottawa. On October 18, 1992, his 16-year-old son, Jesse, was stabbed to death in what was described as a random attack by a group of young people. Cadman and his wife, Dona, responded by forming the group CRY (Crime, Responsibility and Youth). Cadman counselled youth who were prone to violence and also advocated for tougher legislation when it came to youth and crime, a crusade he took to Ottawa when he was first elected to Parliament.

But prior to the 2004 election, Cadman found himself without a party to support him. Jasbir Singh Cheema, a former TV news anchor, had challenged Cadman for the Conservative nomination of Surrey North and won by bringing in a large number of new party members. Still, Cadman decided to run as an Independent to retain his seat. The outcome of the 2004 election was a ringing endorsement for Cadman as the MP for his riding—he secured almost 44 percent of the popular vote, beating the second-place NDP candidate by almost 7000 votes. Cheema finished a distant fourth with 4340 votes.

At that time, Cadman was also facing a personal battle—he had been diagnosed with cancer and had already had one tumour removed from his groin. Heading into the spring budget showdown, Cadman was undergoing chemotherapy for a malignant melanoma.

But the House of Commons was in a peculiar alignment, one that favoured Independent MPs such as Parrish, Kilgour and Cadman. With the vacant Labrador seat, the combined Conservative and Bloc Québécois MPs numbered 153, and the Liberals and NDP numbered 150. So, with the House essentially splitting into two factions in anticipation of a vote on the Liberals' proposed budget, the votes of three Independent MPs were incredibly significant. If one of the three voted against the government on a matter of confidence, such as the budget, the government would fall and Canadians would head back to the polls. Securing all three votes would create a tie, meaning that Speaker Peter Milliken would be forced to vote in order to break the tie.

With Harper declaring his intention to defeat the government, and with the Bloc piling on, that exact scenario began to unfold that April and May as Martin prepared to bring the budget before the House of Commons for a vote. Cadman spoke openly about his intentions—the problem for many was that his intentions kept changing. Cadman said he would listen to the will of his constituents and vote based on that. In the month of April, however, Cadman changed his mind on what he would do, first saying that he would support the Liberals, then saying the following week that constituents had him considering voting against the government.

Cadman's vote became increasingly significant heading into May as Carolyn Parrish made it known that she didn't support holding another election so soon after the last—she intended to vote to support the government. Kilgour was waiting to see what kind of commitment Paul Martin would make to the ongoing conflict in Darfur before deciding how he would vote. And yet Cadman insisted he would continue to listen to constituents until the time came to actually vote.

Cadman's health was also a factor—would he be able to travel in the event of a vote? He wasn't the only MP whose attendance could be impacted by health. Conservative MPs David Chatters (Westlock-St. Paul) and Darrel Stinson (Okanagan-Shuswap) were also being treated for cancer, and early indications were that neither would be able to travel.

No vote on the budget had actually been scheduled yet, but that didn't stop the parties from manoeuvring. Harper kept speaking up, saying he wanted to put the Liberal government "out of its misery." On May 2, Harper emerged from a two-and-a-half-hour caucus meeting and said there was no way the Conservatives could support a government "mired in corruption," alluding to the sponsorship scandal. Conservatives started polling their ridings to gauge the willingness of the electorate for another election. A poll in Cadman's riding showed that 40 percent of respondents did not want another election so soon compared to 29 percent who wanted to bring down the Liberals, while 31 percent did not know how they felt. In anticipation of the vote, Martin began calling back ministers from different trips and events to make sure they were available to vote. That included, much to the anger of some veterans organizations, recalling Veterans Affairs Minister Albina Guarnieri from Holland, where ceremonies celebrating the Second World War Liberation of Holland were taking place.

The Bloc and the Conservatives were growing impatient waiting for Martin to call a vote on the budget, so they decided to try to bring down the government in a different way. On May 9, the Conservatives introduced a motion saying the Liberals had lost the confidence of Parliament, which the Bloc promptly stated it would support. The NDP said it would support the government, but the Liberals refused to take the measure seriously. While the motion said that the Liberals had lost the confidence of the House, the motion in and of itself was not a confidence motion as it did not involve money, and the government had not declared it a matter of confidence. Although the motion was approved by a vote of 153–150, the Liberals simply chose to ignore it.

Martin, however, admitted that the issue of confidence in the government needed to be settled soon and proposed a vote on the budget the following week, on May 19. But for the Conservatives and the Bloc, that wasn't going to be enough. The two opposition parties launched a boycott of the House of Commons. The move denied the government quorum—there weren't enough MPs sitting to conduct even simple business.

Leading up to the vote, the Liberals decided to meet with Chuck Cadman to make their pitch to him and dispatched someone who knew Cadman. Ujjal Dosanjh had been the attorney general for BC when Cadman had worked as a victims' rights advocate. Cadman was open about the fact that he was meeting with the Liberals but said it was unlikely his support could be simply purchased through some kind of deal.

"I'll never say never, but no, I don't believe I can be bought off," Cadman said. "The way things are right now, what's the chances of any offer ever materializing?"

He said that he would do his best to be in the House of Commons for the May 19 vote and maintained, as he had all along, that he would vote based on what his constituents told him.

"The people that want to hold off [on an election] are in the lead, but only by a few points," Cadman said, giving an update as to what his constituents wanted. That reflected what the *Vancouver Sun* reported in a poll of the Surrey North riding—62 percent of respondents said they did not want another election.

The date of the vote angered Conservatives. They revealed that Darrel Stinson, who along with Cadman and David Chatters was being treated for cancer, was scheduled for surgery on May 18, the day before the vote, and would be unable to attend. The Conservatives started launching wild accusations against the Liberals, suggesting that the Liberals were purposely delaying the vote on the budget so that both Chatters and Stinson grew sicker and would be unable to make the vote.

"We're not going to play another week so he can hope the health of some members of Parliament deteriorates," Harper said.

The *National Post* went so far as to report that Liberals were calling around looking for information on Stinson's treatments and that MP Albina Guarnieri, the Minister for Veterans Affairs, had raised the subject during a meeting with Cadman. The *Post* issued an apology and correction the following day, saying that the "allegation is unfounded."

Harper finally instructed Stinson to stay home and recover from his surgery. But in what the NDP called an attempt to restore some form of civility in the House, former NDP leader and sitting MP Ed Broadbent offered to "pair" with Stinson to ensure that Stinson's absence would not impact the vote's outcome. Pairing, in the Parliamentary tradition, is a system in which two members from opposing parties agree to abstain from a vote when one member is unable to vote.

"It seems to me it's a civilized, kind and decent thing to do.... Sometimes there aren't ulterior motives," Broadbent said. "Sometimes people just do things for the right reasons. Someone's very ill, so we aren't going to gain or lose anything by doing this, so the offer was made, and I think it is the right thing to do."

The Liberals, in the end, offered to pair one of their members with Stinson. While at first it appeared that John Efford (Avalon), who was being treated for diabetes, would be paired with Stinson, in the end, Peter Adams (Peterborough) was tapped to abstain from the vote.

But even with the pairing, a Conservative victory in the May 19 vote wasn't assured, even from within the Conservative Party. The proposed Liberal budget contained a $2-billion deal for the Atlantic provinces that would mean hundreds of millions in offshore resource revenues for the province of Newfoundland and Labrador. Two of the province's MPs—Norman Doyle and Loyola Hearn—were Conservatives who could be held partially responsible by voters if the budget was defeated and, with it, the deal for the Atlantic provinces. Newfoundland and Labrador residents started online petitions for the pair to vote for the budget, garnering thousands of signatures. Even feisty and outspoken premier Danny Williams weighed in.

"Depending on how [Hearn and Doyle] vote will depend on whether the budget succeeds or not. So the

Atlantic Accords are in their hands," Williams said at one point.

Leading up to May 19, neither of the two MPs was willing to say how they would vote.

"There are so many things happening, so I'm going to wait for a day or two before actually saying beyond a shadow of a doubt that the budget vote is on today and I'm voting for or against it. I'm just going to play those cards when the time comes around," Doyle said.

If both MPs voted according to the party line, the combined Conservative and Bloc opposition needed only one of the three Independents sitting in the House to defeat the government, and securing at least one of them looked increasingly likely. Paul Martin had finally announced the government's commitment to the ongoing conflict in Darfur—$170 million to send 100 Canadian technical and logistics personnel to the area. Kilgour, who had been waiting for the announcement, promptly deemed the commitment insufficient, paving the way for him to vote with the opposition and bring down the government.

And then late one night in Ottawa, the entire equation changed, and it did not favour the opposition.

Belinda Stronach was the MP for Newmarket-Aurora and a member of the Conservative caucus. The daughter of Frank Stronach, the former president and CEO of Magna International, a substantial auto parts company, had first decided to enter politics at the age of 38 to contest the leadership of the Conservative Party. She captured a significant amount of media and public attention because of her age and attractive looks, as well as her background. Despite the fact that she did not participate in a pair of debates with candidates Stephen Harper and Tony Clement, she still captured 35 percent of the vote, finishing second to Harper. She went on to contest her seat in Newmarket-Aurora and won by only 689 votes. She was seen as different from the vast majority of Conservatives because she supported abortion rights, same-sex marriage and gun control. She and fellow Conservative MP Peter MacKay (Central Nova) were also the talk of the social circuit in Ottawa because they were romantically involved.

But on Wednesday, May 18, one day before the vote on the proposed budget was scheduled to take place, Prime Minister Paul Martin called a press conference and walked into the conference with Stronach behind him. What Martin said next stunned the entire press corps—Stronach was crossing the floor from the Conservative Party caucus to sit as a Liberal member of Parliament.

"I've got to tell you, I can count," Martin joked part way through his statement.

Stronach explained that she was no longer happy as a member of the Conservative Party.

"I've been uncomfortable for some time with the direction the leader of the Conservative Party is taking. I do not believe the party leader is truly sensitive to the needs of each part of the country," Stronach said, referring to Harper. Martin announced that Stronach would receive a cabinet position as Minister of Human Resources, with, as Martin described it, an emphasis on "democratic renewal."

Harper promptly criticized Stronach's decision, saying that he felt she had crossed the floor to the Liberals because she had realized her ambitions to be leader of the Conservative Party would not come to pass.

"I told my wife only a few days ago that I thought it had become obvious to Belinda that her leadership ambitions would not be reached in this party regardless of whether or not we won the next election, that they just weren't in the cards. And I thought that would mean trouble," Harper said. "Frankly, I'm relieved that we've at least gone through this before an election rather than during it."

The relationship between Stronach and MacKay was also over, with Harper describing MacKay as "devastated and quite betrayed."

Stronach's move changed the dynamics of the upcoming vote in the house. Now instead of needing just one of the three Independents to vote against the government, the Conservatives and Bloc Québécois needed two of them. Carolyn Parrish had already made it known she planned to vote with the Liberals. With Kilgour unhappy with the Liberal commitment to Darfur and now likely to vote against the government, that left Cadman as the swing vote. The fate of the Liberal government rested on what the Independent MP from Surrey North decided to do. A new poll in Cadman's riding showed that, of 600 people interviewed, 65 percent did not want another election any time soon. And Cadman maintained that he would not make a decision until he actually sat down in the House of Commons to vote.

The day of the vote was not without drama. First, Liberal MP Jim Karygiannis (Scarborough-Agincourt) was taken away by ambulance complaining of chest pains—it later turned out to be heartburn and he declared that he would be present in the House of Commons for the vote. Then Carolyn Parrish cancelled a morning appearance on CTV's *Canada AM* because of severe abdominal pain. There was originally speculation that the cause was appendicitis, but after being examined by fellow MP and doctor Bernard Patry (Pierrefonds-Dollard), it was determined the pain was caused by either an ovarian cyst or a kidney stone. Parrish, too, vowed she would be in the House of Commons for the vote.

But the Hill was also buzzing from an announcement the previous day—Conservative MP Gurmant Grewal (Newton-North Delta) said that both he and his wife Nina (Fleetwood-Port Kells) had been approached by the Liberals and offered inducements to cross the floor. Specifically, Grewal said that his wife had been offered a seat in the Senate and he was promised a diplomatic posting if they agreed to switch from sitting as Conservatives to sitting as Liberals.

"In exchange, I was given an understanding that I would be rewarded in some fashion," said Grewal.

The Liberals were quick to respond that it was Grewal who had approached them, saying he would cross the floor in exchange for some kind of favourable appointment or posting.

"He indicated he would cross the floor to support the government. I told him that it would be better to abstain on [today's] vote," said Tim Murphy, the prime minister's chief of staff.

But to back up his claim, Grewal revealed that he had taped some of the conversations he had had with the Liberals. The tapes indicated that there were conversations of some kind taking place, but it was difficult to determine exactly who had approached whom.

Rumours were also circulating that another Conservative MP, Lee Richardson (Calgary Centre), had been approached at an upscale Ottawa restaurant by two Liberal cabinet ministers. Richardson, however, denied he had been offered a cabinet posting to switch sides.

"There's no bigger Tory than me. It is preposterous to even suggest that I would consider that. I had no offer and if I had, I wouldn't have given it any consideration," Richardson said.

As the time came for the vote, all MPs filed into the house, except for Stinson, who was recovering from surgery, and Adams, who had been paired with Stinson to cancel out the ill MP's absence.

Cadman looked different from the figure he had cut on Parliament Hill to date. He had cut his long, grey hair to a length just above his shoulders. He was also more than 20 kilograms lighter as a result of his ongoing chemotherapy. As well, he revealed that the Conservatives had tried to sway him to vote in their favour—before the vote in the House, he had said during an interview on the CTV current affairs show *Mike Duffy Live* that the Conservative Party had offered him an uncontested nomination so that he could run as a Conservative in the next election.

"That was the only offer on anything that I had from anybody," Cadman said on the show. "So there was no offers on the table up till that point about anything from any party."

Cadman was also true to his word—he had revealed nothing about how he would vote. The rest of the country watching the vote live on television waited to see what he would do. Kilgour was voting with the opposition, Parrish with the Liberals and the NDP.

The government side of the house erupted in applause and cheers as the gaunt-looking Cadman stood to cast his vote with the Liberals and the NDP. The end result, once all the MPs had been counted, was a 152–152 tie. That left it to Speaker Peter Milliken, a Liberal, to cast the deciding vote, the first time in history that a Speaker of the House of Commons had ever had to break a tie in a confidence vote. Milliken explained that precedent and tradition required him to vote to keep a matter open for further consideration—in this case, that meant approving the second reading of the budget so there could be further debate in third reading. With Milliken's vote, the second reading of the budget was approved 153–152.

In interviews after the vote, Cadman said he made up his mind how he was going to vote about half an hour before he reported to the House of Commons. He stated again that he wasn't given anything in exchange for his vote.

"The only thing I ever demanded was a couple of tickets to Mark Knopfler and a case of beer. But nobody came through with that one," Cadman said jokingly.

After the vote, Justice Minister Irwin Cotler approached Cadman and said he wanted to start moving ahead with more victims' rights work and that he wanted to speak with Cadman about that.

The vote proved to be the edge of the crisis, and from that moment on, the Conservatives started to back away from their threat to defeat the Liberal government and send Canadians back to the polls. Later in June, when 15 different confidence motions came up for a vote in the House of Commons, all passed without the drama that had taken place in May.

On Saturday, July 11, not two months after Chuck Cadman had voted with the Liberals to support their 2005 budget, the Cadman family announced that Chuck had died at his home in the presence of his wife Dona. He was 57 years old. His death was attributed to the skin cancer he had been fighting.

"Cadman," said Prime Minister Paul Martin, "was an outstanding and influential Parliamentarian" who was "drawn to public service by tragedy [and] who made a real and positive difference to Canada's justice system."

Hundreds of people, including the prime minister and Stephen Harper, attended Cadman's memorial service, which was also broadcast live on national television. The flag on Parliament Hill was lowered to half-mast in his honour. On September 29, when Parliament resumed after its summer break, all the MPs in attendance observed a moment of silence for Cadman. Cotler introduced two bills in Cadman's honour that were expected to pass quickly—one that made it a crime to tamper with vehicle identification numbers on cars and a second that imposed stiffer sentences for vehicular crimes such as criminal negligence causing death or bodily harm.

On November 28, 2005, the opposition parties of the House of Commons were finally able to defeat the Liberal government in a vote of confidence, triggering an election. On January 23, 2006, Canadians voted to give Stephen Harper and his Conservatives a minority government, with Harper's team winning 124 of 308 possible seats. The Liberals won 103 seats, and Paul Martin announced he would step down as leader of the party. The Bloc Québécois finished with 51 seats and the NDP with 29. There was also one Independent candidate elected. New Democrat Penny Priddy won Cadman's seat.

Five months after the election, on May 26, Prime Minister Stephen Harper announced that, in honour of Chuck Cadman and after consulting with his widow Dona, the government would introduce legislation allowing stiffer sentences for street racers and prohibitions for those convicted.

But Dona informed the press that she had never been consulted about the legislation, nor had she been told of the announcement, which she dismissed as "typical political bull." She added that she would have liked to have attended if the legislation did indeed honour her husband.

Yet that wasn't the last time Cadman's name would come up on the federal stage. On February 28, 2008, it was reported in the national media that a new biography about Chuck Cadman was about to be released, and in the book, it was stated that two individuals representing the Conservative Party of Canada had met with Cadman two days before the May 2005 vote and offered him a $1 million life insurance policy in exchange for Cadman voting against the government. The book, entitled *Like a Rock: The Chuck Cadman Story*, written by Tom Zytaruk, stated, "The Tories actually walked in with a list of offers written down on a piece of paper. Included in their proposal was a $1 million life insurance policy—no small carrot for a man with advanced cancer."

The information came from Dona Cadman. The book went on to say that the offer enraged Cadman, and he responded by throwing the pair out of his office.

"He just said that he was insulted and that he was ashamed to have been part of the Conservative Party," according to Dona Cadman.

The implications of what Zytaruk reported were significant—offering a sitting member of the government some kind of inducement was a potentially criminal act under two different pieces of legislation. Section 119 of the Criminal Code of Canada makes bribery an offence punishable by up to 14 years in prison, while the Parliament of Canada Act provides for up to one year in prison for illegal compensation to a member of Parliament.

What made the allegations even more awkward was that Dona Cadman was now the Conservative nominee to run for her husband's old seat.

Harper was quick to deny what was in the book, with the Prime Minister's Office issuing a statement saying that Harper "at no time directed any party official to make any kind of financial arrangement with Chuck Cadman."

Zytaruk had actually spoken with Stephen Harper on September 9, 2005; Harper paid Dona Cadman a visit at her home, and Zytaruk was present. At that time, while standing in the Cadmans' driveway, Zytaruk asked Harper about the story.

According to the book, Harper replied that the offer "was only to replace financial considerations he might lose due to an election.... That's my understanding of what they were talking about."

According the statement from the PMO, "The then-leader of the opposition looked into the matter with party officials and could find no confirmation." At the time, Harper was still the leader of the opposition and not prime minister. "And that is the last time he heard anything regarding this matter."

There were some problems with the story, the first of which was that it was difficult to believe any insurance company would be willing to give a man with terminal cancer a $1 million life insurance policy. That suspicion was confirmed by brokers interviewed by the media.

But the opposition parties were in an uproar over the allegations and requested that both the RCMP and the House's own ethics committee investigate the matter.

The Conservatives responded by producing two of their own advisors who said they had met with Cadman. Tom Flanagan and Doug Finley both said they had spoken to Cadman, but the only thing they had offered him was that he could win the next Conservative nomination in his riding without it being contested "and a competitive campaign in a general election."

That, however, was also difficult to believe for members of the opposition. They asserted that if Cadman was, in fact, "at death's door" as many said, there was no way he was going to run in another election, so the offer by Flanagan and Finley made no sense. The opposition attacked Harper during Question Period with the statement about the supposed offer to Cadman.

Harper replied, "These allegations are completely false and irresponsible," but when deputy Liberal leader Michael Ignatieff asked if Harper was saying that Dona Cadman was lying, Harper declined to respond. Meanwhile, the RCMP confirmed that they had received a request from the Liberals to investigate the allegations.

The Conservatives zeroed in on a clip of Chuck Cadman on TV to try to prove that what the book was saying was untrue. They reminded everyone of the clip from *Mike Duffy Live* that aired before the May 2005 budget vote in which Cadman said that the only thing he was offered was an uncontested election.

"Chuck Cadman himself on national television on the day of that historic vote also indicated that the story is not true, so I wish everybody would accept his word," Harper said.

Yet Dona Cadman, in subsequent media interviews, confirmed what was written in the book. Jodi Cadman, her daughter, also vouched for the story, saying her father didn't want to reveal the offer publicly because he felt the resulting storm of publicity would have been too much for him to handle, being as sick as he was.

"All of this, this circus, would have been happening for the last weeks of his life," Jodi said. "What would they want, cameras around his deathbed? He didn't want that. He was dying."

Jodi's husband, Holland Miller, backed up his wife, saying that after the 2005 vote, Cadman "did specifically tell me this offer was made. He said a million-dollar life insurance policy. Now, I know that doesn't make a lot of sense to what people are saying, but that's exactly what he said."

A tape containing the interview between Zytaruk and Harper was finally released and was immediately met with criticism as being an edited version of a longer conversation. Zytaruk maintained that it was unedited, that one small break in the sound happened when Harper went to his car and then returned to add a comment while the two were standing in the driveway. The tape contained the quote already attributed to Harper in the book that "the offer to Chuck was that it was only to replace financial considerations he might lose due to an election."

In March 2008, Dona Cadman issued a statement saying that she believed Harper knew nothing of the offer. Posted on her website, Dona was quoted as saying, "[Harper] looked me straight in the eyes and told me he had no knowledge of an insurance policy offer. I knew he was telling me the truth: I could see it in his eyes."

Dona Cadman's statement came just as the Conservative Party issued a notice of a libel action against the Liberal Party and its leader, Stéphane Dion, claiming that Harper had been libelled in two articles posted on the Liberal website. The notice called on the Liberals to remove both articles from the website and for Dion to issue an apology to Harper. The Liberals responded by saying they would not back down.

As the scandal continued to unfold, the book's publisher announced a change to the manuscript, saying it would delete references to May 17, 2005, the date the offer was allegedly made, because according to publisher Howard White, "we simply don't know." Cadman's former assistant was quoted as saying there was only one meeting that took place with Flanagan and Finley, and it took place on May 19.

There was also drama outside Question Period, within the meetings of the justice committee. Chaired by Conservative Art Hanger (Calgary Northeast), a majority of the committee wanted to vote in favour of holding hearings into the Cadman affair. As chair, Hanger was not permitted to vote unless it was to break a tie, and the Conservatives on the committee were outnumbered by opposition members. Rather than call for a vote on the motion, Hanger proceeded to walk out of the committee, not just once, but during three separate meetings. With no chair, a vote could not be called. Furthermore, the Liberal vice-chair refused to sit in Hanger's place because it would mean he would not be able to vote, and the motion would have failed.

"I will not let this committee turn into a circus," Hanger said as he walked out the second time.

The opposition members threatened to have Hanger removed as chair, but Hanger said it would be up to the Speaker to intervene. Milliken later issued a statement, calling for an end to the "anarchy" taking place in several committees.

On March 14, the Conservatives officially sued the Liberals for libel, seeking $2.5 million in damages. The libel, according to the suit, consisted of statements in two articles on the Liberal website in which was written that Harper knew of the alleged bribery attempt. In their statement of defence, the Liberals replied that the lawsuit was a "fundamental attack on freedom of political expression," and called for the suit to be dismissed.

The matter moved into the courtroom, but not before the Conservatives added $1 million in damages to their claim, citing "misappropriation of personality" and also filed an injunction against continued use of the tape of Zytaruk's interview with Harper. Once lawyers started filing affidavits, more information started to come out. First was the affidavit of Dona Cadman, who went so far as to say that Zytaruk did not meet Harper in the Cadman house as claimed, and that Dona had not introduced the two.

"Nobody came inside my house while Mr. Harper was in the house with me. I did not introduce Tom Zytaruk to Mr. Harper on September 9, 2005," Dona stated in her affidavit.

Zytaruk replied publicly by saying that not only was he at the house when Harper was there, but also that after he interviewed Harper, he went inside and played the tape of the interview for Dona.

It was the tape that proved to be at issue in court filings. First came statements in affidavits filed by Harper and two aides in which they stated that Zytaruk did not turn his recorder on and off during the interview. Zytaruk had said turning it on and off had caused some breaks in the audio. The Tories said the sounds were those of the tape being edited.

The tape had been submitted by the Tories for testing by two experts, but one was forced to back away from one of his statements. Alan Gough had initially concluded that the sound of someone saying "um" on the tape was Zytaruk, while Tom Owen, another expert, said Harper had made the utterance. Gough later explained his finding that Zytaruk had made the sound was "a matter of convenience," that he was not asked to analyze the voices on the tape and that had he been asked, he would have refused because he didn't "hold myself out to be qualified in this specific area of audio analysis."

The judge in the case requested that a court-supervised analysis of the tape be performed. In October 2008, the audio expert tapped by Harper to perform that analysis said the tape was not doctored and the portion of the tape with Harper speaking contained "neither physical nor electronic splices, edits or alterations," according to a report filed with the court.

On October 16, Dona Cadman was declared the winner of her husband's seat, having run under the Conservative banner.

But there were few other developments in the lawsuit or the issue of the alleged offer to Chuck Cadman. While some members of the Harper legal team changed over, it was announced in February 2009 that a settlement of the suit had been reached by both sides and the case was dismissed. No details on the settlement were made public, and no comment was given in response to questions as to whether or not there was any financial compensation involved in the settlement.

CHAPTER TWO

In-and-Out Scandal

THE ELECTION OF 2006 brought the Conservatives what they had been working toward since the twin parties of the old Progressive Conservatives and the Canadian Alliance merged—they were able to form a government. It wasn't a majority government—the Conservatives had won a plurality of seats, but had come short of a majority, meaning that the combined seats held by the opposition parties exceeded what the Conservatives had won. Their minority status meant the Conservatives would have to govern carefully.

The Conservatives had, however, been successful in getting rid of Paul Martin. The leader of the Liberal Party had announced his resignation shortly after the election. The Liberal defeat had been largely attributed to the fallout from the sponsorship scandal that had rocked the country under Martin's tenure as prime minister.

Election law in Canada, particularly as it relates to spending, is pretty rigorous. What many of the laws try to do is create parity between the parties—a level playing field. Elections Canada reimburses most eligible campaign expenses for about 60 percent of total expenditures. Parties that reach a certain vote threshold also receive a per-vote subsidy, which at the time hovered between $1.79 and $1.83 per vote. Based on the results of the 2006 election, as an example, the Conservatives would receive approximately $9.775 million in per-vote subsidies, while the Liberals would get about $8.148 million.

There are several limits on how money can be used when it comes to running a political party or contesting an election. There is a cap on individual and corporate donations, limiting how much a person or a business can donate to a party in one year. When elections come around, there are limits on what parties are allowed to spend nationally and on what individual candidates are allowed to spend locally in an election. Exceeding those limits can lead to the party being penalized under the Elections Act by way of a fine or a jail term. All expenses need to be filed with Elections Canada in order to receive the 60 percent rebate and to ensure that spending limits aren't exceeded.

But when Elections Canada officials started going through the expense claims of several dozen Conservative candidates, both successful and not, from the 2006 election, they noticed some oddities. There were several campaigns that were claiming expenses for purchasing broadcast advertising in their ridings, which at first glance was legitimate. But for a lot of the ads purchased, it was difficult to tell exactly who the advertising was for. The ads were strikingly similar to the ads purchased by the national campaign that promoted Stephen Harper and the Conservatives. The only difference between the ads purchased by these candidates and the ads purchased by the national campaign was the tagline at the end of each one. That line typically stated who had authorized the commercial. The name in that tagline changed depending on the riding in which the ad aired.

As Elections Canada officials probed the expense claims a little more, they found that these campaigns, roughly 67 in total, had all received wire transfers from the national party that were then returned—usually within a matter of minutes—to the national party. The transfers to and from these ridings totalled approximately $1.3 million. And those transfers were used to purchase broadcast advertising in the local ridings, using the ads that so closely resembled the national ads.

Elections Canada also noted a few other seeming coincidences among these transfers. First, they occurred at a time when the national party had reached the spending limit that Elections Canada had imposed on all of the national campaigns—$18.3 million. They also noticed that the 67 individual campaigns that accepted and returned the transfers that were used to buy the ads all had a relatively healthy balance remaining in their accounts and were not in danger of exceeding the $80,000 limit imposed on individual campaigns.

What appeared to have happened, in the eyes of Chief Electoral Officer Marc Maynard, was that the national Conservative campaign in the 2006 election had gotten around the $18.3 million spending limit for national campaigns by transferring money to individual campaigns, taking it back, and then having the individual campaigns record it as their advertising expense. Those invoices were then submitted to Elections Canada for the 60 percent rebate. Essentially, if Elections Canada did not allow those expenses, it would mean that the Conservative Party would have spent $1.3 million more than the national spending limit and would have broken Canadian election law.

In the end, Maynard chose not to reimburse the individual campaigns for those advertising expenses. In response, the Conservative Party launched a lawsuit against Elections Canada to try to get their money back. In court documents filed in August 2007, Elections Canada claimed that agents for candidates were claiming expenses for advertising that Elections Canada did not feel could be proven were for the candidates themselves. The Conservatives replied by saying that all the expenses were legitimate and that each ad that ran in a candidate's riding carried that candidate's tagline at the end. But the Tories had experienced a few issues with their candidates when it came to the types of ads that ran—there were ridings in which the ads attacked the Liberal Party even though the Conservatives' chief opponent in that riding was actually the NDP.

The Tories also claimed that transfers between the national party and individual ridings were perfectly legal and were, in fact, common. The party even produced a list of seven Liberal candidates who, during the 2006 election, had received transfers from the national Liberal campaign. The difference, as the Liberal Party was quick to point out, was that the totals transferred between the Liberal candidates and the national campaign were much smaller than the money moved around by the Conservatives.

In a letter to Elections Canada, the Conservatives tried to explain what had happened as a group media buy—that all 67 ridings agreed to buy regional advertising using Toronto-based media buyer Retail Media, and they purchased $1.3 million in regional advertising.

Yet Elections Canada found at least one candidate and an agent for another candidate who had no knowledge of any advertising purchases using the party's media buyer.

The Liberals, perhaps sensitive to any kind of financial scandal given the sponsorship scandal that had knocked them out of power, began to pressure the Conservatives over the Elections Canada allegations.

"The Conservative Party appears to have found a scheme to make Elections Canada and Canadian taxpayers recoup advertising expenses allegedly done by local campaigns, which, in fact, may have been done for the benefit of the national party," said New Brunswick MP Dominic LeBlanc.

The Conservatives even filed an affidavit in the court case in November 2007 in which the party cited 100 cases involving the Liberal Party, the Bloc Québécois and the NDP transferring money between the national campaign and individual candidates. Elections Canada, however, charged that the transfers in which the Conservative Party engaged were not meant to actually financially assist individual candidates, but were instead used to buy ads that promoted the party on the national level.

While Elections Canada and the Conservatives fought it out in court in response to the Conservatives' lawsuit trying to compel the government body to repay the money spent, Elections Canada was conducting a separate investigation in an attempt to determine whether or not the Conservatives had broken the Canada Elections Act by exceeding the $18.3 million spending limit. That investigation led, on April 16, 2008, to election officials, with help from the RCMP, executing a search warrant on the Conservatives' Ottawa headquarters. The Conservatives were particularly irate because someone had tipped off the media, and cameras and reporters were camped outside as the warrant was being executed. Elections Canada made it clear that they had asked for and were executing the search warrant, and that they had merely called on the RCMP to assist them. The search netted several boxes worth of what would later become contentious evidence.

Prime Minister Stephen Harper tried to explain the raid as being somehow linked to the ongoing lawsuit between the party and Elections Canada. The Liberal Party, however, criticized the Conservatives for being at fault.

"This is what we get when we play fast and loose with election law. This is what we get when we stonewall Elections Canada. This is what we get when we cheat and we get caught," said deputy leader Michael Ignatieff.

Harper described as "completely false" any kind of allegation that his party had somehow broken the law.

"This is the reason why the Conservative Party itself has initiated the court action, and obviously we will abide by whatever the courts decide, but in this case our legal position is rock solid," Harper said.

Names were starting to emerge as well—names of the 67 candidates who had received and returned transfers from the national Conservative campaign. Many were unsuccessful candidates, but there were some notable cabinet ministers involved. Included in that list were Foreign Affairs Minister Lawrence Cannon, Treasury Board president Stockwell Day, Natural Resources Minister Christian Paradis, Intergovernmental

Affairs Minister Josée Verner and former Foreign Affairs Minister Maxime Bernier.

The Conservatives criticized Elections Canada on two levels—first, they alleged that Elections Canada had tipped off the media about the search of the Conservative headquarters. The Conservatives also claimed that prior to the search, it had been roughly three months since anyone from Elections Canada had requested anything from the party. Elections Canada responded that it had asked 14 different Conservative officials and candidates for documents that would disprove the allegations of what was now being described as the "in-and-out" scheme. When none of those individuals co-operated, Elections Canada went out and got their search warrant. In their application to a judge for the warrant, Elections Canada filed almost 800 pages in supporting documentation.

The following week, the Conservatives tried to manage the message for the media. The result was something of a farce. Since taking power, the Conservatives had played favourites with the media, much to the chagrin of the press gallery on Parliament Hill. In this case, Conservative Party spokesperson Ryan Sparrow called a select few media organizations to a secret meeting at the Lord Elgin Hotel with himself, Doug Finley, the Conservatives' campaign organizer, and a party lawyer, to discuss the allegations that the Conservative Party had violated the Canada Elections Act and to show those invited some documents associated with the case. Media who had not been invited to the meeting, however, quickly found out its location and when it was taking place. Sparrow switched the location of the meeting to the Sheraton Hotel, but that location also leaked to the press who had not been invited.

What ensued was something of a circus as the media who had not been invited clustered outside the doors of the room at the Sheraton where the meeting was taking place and tried to look through the peepholes. They were asked to leave the building but refused. When the meeting broke up early, before any of those inside had a chance to look at the promised documents, a rather surreal scene ensued as journalists started interviewing other journalists while Sparrow and Finley tried to escape out the fire exits.

There were documents for everyone to see later as the 800 pages used to justify the search warrants were perused by the media. Some of those documents revealed concern on the part of those involved in purchasing ads that what they were doing might not be entirely legal. One representative of Retail Media, the party's media buyer during the campaign, was quoted in an email as wondering if their placing ads on behalf of local candidates was a violation of the Canada Elections Act.

"While our thinking is that this option would be legal, we are not certain beyond all reasonable doubt," the representative wrote.

There had even been some issues with purchases. In one case, the CBC had replied to a request for advertising that it couldn't take orders that Retail Media placed for local candidates because Retail Media wasn't actually an agent for any of the local campaigns.

One email from a Conservative official to local riding leaders explained what was happening.

"This is a transfer in and then back out, same day. You will still be able to use the 60 percent [rebate from Elections Canada] you will get back from this amount after filing election expenses in whatever way your team desires," Brian Hudson wrote.

Barbro Soderberg, an official agent for Conservative Steven Halicki, expressed some concern about the move in an email.

"As a bookkeeper, I know that sometimes you have to use creative accounting between two small companies, but I found this move was being a little too creative," Soderberg wrote.

One candidate based in Victoria had fired off an angry email that was also included in Election Canada's records about the fact that the ads that ran in one candidate's riding were anti-Liberal, when that individual was facing the most competition from an NDP candidate.

"They have heard the first ad running, and it is an anti-[Liberal] ad and they are really pissed off, since the Liberals are not a factor [in] and of the three [ridings] in their area," wrote a lawyer complaining to the Conservative national campaign about the ads.

"The Liberals continue to poll well on Vancouver Island regardless of what we are seeing on the ground," Patrick Muttart, a Tory strategist, replied. "We do have an anti-NDP ad for television that is being finalized."

The House of Commons ethics committee, free now of a months-long filibuster that had been stalling plans for a hearing, voted in June to start holding hearings on the matter. It was a compelling prospect—a Parliamentary committee potentially hauling the prime minister before it to answer questions about the in-and-out financing scheme.

But while the committee tried to call witnesses, few of the Conservatives called chose to respond, or at least conveniently found reasons to be absent. The committee issued summons to several individuals but failed to accomplish much. Doug Finley was summoned to testify on a Wednesday in August but instead appeared on a Monday, explaining that he had been unavailable on the Wednesday. The committee said it could not hear his testimony out of turn and asked him to leave. Finley and his lawyer refused, sitting in place for roughly six minutes before security showed up to escort the two out.

The following day, four campaign agents who had been called to testify failed to show up, while the day after that, 11 Conservatives scheduled to appear before the committee failed to appear. On Thursday, August 14, Sam Goldstein, the defeated Conservative candidate for the Trinity-Spadina riding in Toronto, showed up to testify, but the committee refused to hear his testimony. He had been scheduled to testify on the Tuesday, but hadn't received his summons until late Monday and claimed he did not have time to make the trip to Ottawa. When the committee refused to let Goldstein testify, Goldstein became angry and started shouting, demanding that the committee hear what he had to say.

The committee ultimately accomplished little, which put a heightened sense of importance on what was happening in the courts and with Elections Canada, as far as the opposition was concerned.

In January 2009, the Conservatives took the issue of the 2008 raid on Conservative headquarters to court, telling an Ontario Superior Court judge in an application that Elections Canada had taken a large volume of documentation that had little to do with the reasons for the search that were specified on the warrant. Investigators had carted away many boxes of documentation and computer hard drives, netting millions of documents, many of which contained information the Conservatives said had nothing to do with the case at hand. The Conservatives also argued that a great deal of what had been taken was covered by solicitor-client privilege, meaning it could only be viewed by party officials or their lawyers. Elections Canada replied that the privilege issue was interfering with the investigation and asked for a court hearing to determine what was covered and what was not.

Documents from the 2008 election, however, hinted that the Conservatives had dropped their "in-and-out" scheme altogether. Of the 192 Conservative candidates who had their expense reports published following the 2008 election, none showed that they had funnelled their broadcast advertising buys through the national party, as they had in 2006. In fact, average spending in the 2008 campaign on radio and TV advertising by Conservative ridings had dropped 40 percent compared to the 2006 election, according to a *National Post* report.

It appeared in January 2010 that the Conservatives had scored a win in their ongoing battle with Elections Canada. The Federal Court of Canada ordered Chief Electoral Officer Marc Mayrand to allow two Tory candidates to claim their expenses for their 2006 broadcast advertising purchases. The two cases were looked upon as a test for the remaining 65 candidates who had taken part in the in-and-out scheme. In his ruling, Justice Luc Martineau concluded that the expenses had been incurred by the candidates, and as such, they should be allowed to claim them. Martineau strongly urged, however, that his finding did not necessarily have anything to do with the ongoing Elections Canada investigation.

"There is a fundamental distinction between legality and legitimacy," Judge Martineau wrote in his decision. "As far as the overall legitimacy of the [regional media buy] program is concerned, this is a debatable issue, which is better left for public commentary and debate by all interested persons outside the courts."

The Conservatives hailed it as a victory that should exonerate them. But that February, Elections Canada announced that it was appealing the ruling. Everyone involved, including Judge Martineau, had believed that an appeal of his ruling, even if he had ruled for Elections Canada, was likely.

It took one more year, but in February 2011, Elections Canada formally announced charges against the Conservative Party and four of its officials over the in-and-out scheme that had taken place during the 2006 election. The four officials were Doug Finley, the party's campaign director in 2006 and 2008; Irving Gerstein, a party fundraiser; Michael Donnison, a former national party director; and Susan Kehoe, who had served as interim party executive director. The charges included allegations that the party and its fundraising arm deliberately filed false or misleading statements from the 2006 election, and that the party had surpassed the imposed national limit on election spending in the 2006 election. Of note were the facts that Finley and Gerstein were now sitting Conservative senators, and that Kehoe now worked for the Auditor General of Canada. The office clarified, however, that Kehoe worked with the Canadian Council of Legislative Auditors, a body that is run from a secretariat within the office of the Auditor General, and she had no role in reviewing government expenses.

One month after the charges were filed, the Conservatives suffered another setback when the Federal Court of Appeal overturned Judge Martineau's January 2010 ruling to allow two candidates to claim their expenses. In its ruling, the court said that the chief electoral officer was acting within his rights to disallow the advertising expenses of those candidates. It was his right, the court argued, to question all expenses incurred by candidates.

The Liberals seized on the ruling.

"[The ruling] has completely demolished the rather silly defence that the PM and his MPs have been using with respect to the quasi-criminal charges," said LeBlanc. He further added that the Conservatives were "wrong to try to milk taxpayers' refunds for a scheme that was designed to get around advertising spending limits."

In November 2011, the Conservative Party reached a deal with Elections Canada and the courts over the charges under the Canada Elections Act. In exchange for dropping charges against Finley, Gerstein, Donnison and Kehoe, the party and its fundraising branch, the Conservative Fund, pleaded guilty to charges of exceeding the maximum allowable election expenses and to filing records that did not include all expenses. The charges against the party and the fund of "wilfully" breaking both laws, considered more serious, were withdrawn. As penalty for the guilty plea, the party was fined the maximum allowable $50,000 and the fund $2000.

The Conservatives, of course, hailed what happened in court as a "victory."

"This is a big victory for the Conservative Party of Canada," Party spokesperson Fred DeLorey said in a written statement. "Every single Conservative accused of wrongdoing has been cleared today."

Less than six months later, the in-and-out scandal effectively ended when the Conservatives announced they were dropping their appeal of the Federal Court of Appeal's ruling the previous year. That ruling had overturned a lower court ruling that Elections Canada allow two candidates to claim their broadcast advertising expenses. The Conservatives had been seeking leave to appeal to the Supreme Court of Canada, but said they would now drop that appeal. The party also agreed to repay $230,198 in taxpayer dollars.

"We are agreeing to disagree and will be dropping our appeal to the Supreme Court. We are amending our return under protest to reflect this," said DeLorey in a written statement.

"The Conservative Party of Canada plays by the same rules as everyone else; we acted under the law as it was understood at that time," he added.

CHAPTER THREE

Afghan Detainee Affair

THE WAR IN Afghanistan was, for many Canadians, the first large-scale conflict that they had any personal connection to. The Canadian Forces had taken part in their share of conflicts around the world but had primarily operated in a peacekeeping capacity.

The war in Afghanistan was different. It was a sustained, multi-year conflict that had no real peacekeeping component. It was a war, but a different kind of war than those in which Canada had participated in the past—the two World Wars and the Korean War. The enemy was not another country, but a band of like-minded individuals who had once ruled the country—the Taliban. There were no pitched battles featuring tens of thousands of troops because the Taliban were smaller in number and preferred to strike in small groups when they had the element of surprise. The Canadian Forces were waging a war against terrorists.

The conflict in Afghanistan was also the longest war in Canada's history—Canada's commitment lasted from when it first deployed soldiers from Joint Task Force 2 shortly after the attacks of September 11, 2001, until the end of combat operations in 2011, when most of the Canadian troops deployed to Kandahar were brought back home. A smaller group of soldiers stayed in Afghanistan until March 2014 to help with the training of the Afghan National Army. The war claimed the lives of 158 Canadian soldiers, one diplomat, one Canadian journalist and three civilian workers.

For Canadians back home, and for the federal parties in Ottawa, one issue became a source of scandal for the governing Conservatives, and that had to do with the enemy combatants that Canada took into custody. Specifically, there were concerns about how those detainees were treated once Canada handed them over to the authorities in Afghanistan and whether or not the detainees were being abused or tortured.

The issue of the treatment of detainees was a sensitive one for Canadians. For some, the memory of the Somalia Affair still lingered in the national conscience. In that controversy, two Canadian soldiers serving as members of the Canadian Airborne Regiment in Somalia in 1993 tortured and killed a Somali teenager, going so far as to document their abuse in photographs. The scandal became a source of shame for Canada and played a role in the disbanding of the Canadian Airborne Regiment.

This new scandal began to unfold in February 2007 as allegations of the abuse of detainees began to emerge. They stemmed from an access to information request from a professor at the University of Ottawa. Those documents, it was later argued, showed that prisoners might have been abused after they were arrested in southern Afghanistan the previous April. Specifically, the documents stated that three Afghan detainees had similar upper-body injuries, but there was no description of how those injuries had been inflicted.

Two inquiries were launched as a result of the complaints, one by the Forces' own National Investigative Service and another as a board of inquiry convened by Chief of the Defence Staff Rick Hillier. The inquiry, however, was to take place behind closed doors. The fact that it took the military approximately 10 months to investigate the matter was a source of concern for Peter Tinsley, who was the chair of the Military Police Complaints Commission (MPCC). Within weeks of the incident coming to light, based on a complaint by Amnesty International Canada and the BC Civil Liberties Association, Tinsley announced that the MPCC would also investigate, as there were now allegations that the three detainees had been abused by Canadian soldiers. Tinsley also said that he had preliminary information that, on at least 18 occasions, Canadian soldiers had transferred detainees to the Afghan authorities, "notwithstanding alleged evidence there was a likelihood they would be tortured."

The possibility that Canadian troops were handing individuals over to Afghan authorities despite the possibility they would be abused or tortured was problematic for Canada. There was first a moral component on Canada's part, as torture and abuse are generally considered repugnant. But there was also a legal problem. Canada is a signatory to the Geneva Convention, which establishes standards of international law for the humanitarian treatment of prisoners of war. The Third Geneva Convention says that the country that detains a prisoner of war is responsible for the treatment of that prisoner. Essentially, if Canada was handing its prisoners over to be tortured, it could be guilty of war crimes—a very serious charge.

When asked about the possible abuse of detainees by the Afghan authorities, Gordon O'Connor, then serving as the Minister of Defence in the Conservative cabinet, replied by saying that Canada had an agreement in place with the International Committee of the Red Cross (ICRC) to monitor the well-being of detainees.

"The president of the Red Cross also said that basically our procedures are absolutely spotless," O'Connor told reporters. "He's quite pleased with what we do with prisoners."

There was a problem with O'Connor's statement, which the ICRC was quick to explain—the ICRC did not have any role in monitoring the well-being of Afghan detainees under the agreement between Canada and Afghanistan governing such transfers. The opposition was livid after hearing the ICRC's explanation and was quick to call for O'Connor's resignation, claiming that he was either deliberately misleading the House of Commons or he was incompetent.

"At the time, my understanding was the Red Cross was going to inform us. I've subsequently learned that they will not inform us, they inform the Afghan government. But we've got in place another monitoring system with the Human Rights Commission here in Afghanistan," O'Connor later explained.

The second part of his explanation was correct. Canada did have an agreement in place with the Human Rights Commission in Afghanistan to follow up with detainees transferred from Canadian custody to Afghan custody and to ensure that they were treated properly and not tortured or abused. O'Connor even went so far as to travel to Afghanistan to meet with the head of the commission. After a few days of missed meetings and miscommunication, O'Connor was finally able to meet with Abdul Noorzai, head of the Afghanistan Independent Human Rights Commission. The procedure for dealing with detainees was explained further. Basically, when Canadian soldiers took an individual into custody, that individual was brought to the Canadian base at Kandahar Airfield. Canadian troops then had 96 hours to question the individual before either setting that person free or handing the individual over to the Afghan authorities.

In the previous year, Canada had held 85 individuals at the airfield. Stories were starting to emerge that three detainees who had come through the detention centre before being transferred to Afghani custody had simply disappeared and had not been located. It was Noorzai's job to follow up on detainees, but he was quick to ask O'Connor for more help in doing his job because he had a large region to cover. Although O'Connor refused to offer any kind of monetary assistance, he promised more help for Noorzai in getting around the country.

"If some of our detainees are moved to, let's say, a detention centre 50 kilometres from here and he can't get there, we will help him get there, we will give him the transportation to get him there and support him," O'Connor said.

But when O'Connor returned to Canada, the opposition was still calling for his head. O'Connor offered an apology on March 19, 2007, in the House of Commons, stating, "I fully and without reservation apologize to the House for providing inaccurate information to members. I regret any confusion that may have resulted from these statements. The answers I gave were provided in good faith. I take full responsibility and do so without hesitation." He also tabled several documents in the House to correct what he had said.

But the criticisms didn't stop there. New allegations surfaced that O'Connor was now trying to interfere with the MPCC's inquiry into the growing detainee affair. The Department of National Defence had sent a letter to the MPCC, questioning the need for its inquiry.

"I am not interfering with any investigation," O'Connor said. Prime Minister Stephen Harper chose to reply to opposition calls for O'Connor's resignation by suggesting that the Liberal Party had "passion" for the Taliban and not for Canada's own troops. When called to apologize, Harper refused. The next day, when Michael Ignatieff asked again for the Conservatives to apologize, Conservative House Leader Peter Van Loan suggested that Ignatieff approved of torture, based on his previous writings.

"The irony drips," Van Loan said. "The [comment] is from the member for Etobicoke-Lakeshore, who said that torture is justified when dealing with terrorists."

Ignatieff called for Van Loan to apologize, but he refused to do so.

The detainee issue continued to dominate discussions in the House of Commons. Liberal leader Stéphane Dion mused one day about whether or not it was worthwhile to simply bring prisoners from Afghanistan back to Canada, but later backed off that idea, saying it wasn't realistic.

"It's very unlikely that the most practical way to do so is to bring them to Canada, but we cannot give them to the Afghan authorities, so I guess they will need to stay within our Kandahar facilities," Dion said.

The opposition parties started calling for an immediate end to all prisoner transfers between Canada and Afghanistan, but Harper refused to do so, saying his government would examine the issue.

"We have believed that this deal couldn't work because the organization that's supposed to supervise detainees, make sure there isn't mistreatment, hasn't got the resources to do the job," said NDP leader Jack Layton. "That means Canada has a responsibility to ensure that international law is respected with regard to their treatment, and the allegations we see now open Canada to serious accusations in the international community."

O'Connor continued to call allegations of detainee abuse by Afghan authorities "rumours." Harper kept refusing to ask for O'Connor's resignation. But the "rumours" now included specific allegations of beatings, electrical shocks and other abuse at the hands of the intelligence police of the Afghan National Directorate of Security.

In a speech to a group of anti-terror experts on April 24, 2007, Stockwell Day said that the idea of observing human rights in Afghanistan was new for the people of that country:

> *This is a priority for us. In many ways, this is a new area for them, the proper care and respect for prisoners, for instance. For some people, that's kind of a new concept. And they're learning it. It's not moving as quickly as we would have hoped, but progress is being made and we are going to continue to insist that the human rights of everybody, even people who are being detained, are respected.*

The next day, Gordon O'Connor had something else to say about the detainee issue, and it seemed to catch the rest of his Conservative cabinet colleagues by surprise. On April 25, while testifying before the House of Commons Foreign Affairs Committee, O'Connor said that Canada had just completed a new transfer agreement with the Afghan government that would guard against possible incidents of torture and abuse.

"Within the last few days, we have basically made an arrangement with the government in the Kandahar province so that we can have access to our detainees. So henceforth, our military, but it can be anybody, can have access to our detainees," O'Connor told the committee.

But that was all O'Connor was willing to say. Pressed for more information about this new agreement, O'Connor became agitated, suddenly declared he had no time for "histrionics" and fled the committee room without speaking to reporters.

Instead of providing clarity on the issue, it appeared that O'Connor had befuddled the Conservative government. When asked about it, Peter MacKay, the Minister of Foreign Affairs, whom one might assume would be a part of any new deal between Canada and Afghanistan, could add little new detail, telling reporters he had just learned of it.

"Having just heard about it myself, do I think it's a good idea? Sure. Do I think that we will pursue any steps that will put in place a greater sense of accountability and transparency on the part of the Afghans? That's why we put our faith in the Afghan Human Rights Commission," MacKay told reporters.

Even Rick Hillier, the Chief of the Defence Staff and Canada's top soldier, was skeptical of what O'Connor had said, saying that there was no way actual soldiers would be responsible for that kind of monitoring.

"That's not our area of expertise. It wouldn't be soldiers," Hillier said.

O'Connor's office quickly issued a short statement about the new agreement, but the words "Canadian military officials" was changed to "Canadian government officials."

The media continued to ask questions, finally calling O'Connor's office to ask for a copy of the new agreement. That's when an aide unknowingly dropped another bombshell—the media could not have a copy of the agreement because it had not yet been finalized and was still being negotiated.

If the uproar over O'Connor's original misstatement about the role of the ICRC had been loud, then the howling of the opposition over this latest incident was deafening. After all, while one could accept that O'Connor had merely misspoken about the ICRC, to flagrantly state that an agreement that was still being negotiated was, in fact, a *fait accompli* bordered on outright deception and dishonestly.

Stockwell Day then followed up with another strange disclosure, saying that Corrections Canada officials—individuals who worked in Canada's own prison system—had already made 15 visits to Afghan prisons. That marked the first time such information had been made public.

Stephen Harper tried to put a positive spin on it, saying, "We will conclude a formal agreement so that we never again have to face these kinds of baseless accusations," but the opposition was out for blood. Specifically, it wanted O'Connor fired.

"There is an apparent cover-up. It may, in fact, as far as I can see, involve dishonesty. It may involve contempt. It may involve incompetence. It also may be all three," said Liberal MP Paul Szabo (Mississauga South).

As Canada's politicians continued to argue over the issue of detainees and their possible abuse and torture, Afghanistan finally decided to speak up. In a letter to Omar Samad, Afghanistan's ambassador to Canada, Amrullah Saleh, head of the National Directorate of Security, wrote that Afghanistan's jailers took their jobs very seriously and did not deserve the kind of questions over their conduct that were being raised in Canada.

Those workers, Saleh wrote, were "patriots who risk their lives on a daily basis to provide security for the people of Afghanistan. At the end of the month, they get 4800 Afghanis, or $80. They should be praised, not punished."

Saleh went on to write that anyone from Canada's embassy was free at any time to visit detention facilities to interview any detainees they wanted for as long as they wished. He extended the same offer to the Afghanistan Independent Human Rights Commission, which was charged with following up on detainees transferred from Canadian custody to the Afghanis. He admitted in his letter that, when jailers moved detainees, they chained them and secured their hands, but asked, "Do Canadians have any other method of how we should transport these detainees from one place to another?"

But Canada wasn't alone in its concern over how Afghanistan treated its prisoners. The United Nations High Commissioner for Human Rights had recently issued a report that alleged incidents of detention without trial, extortion, torture and violations of the due process of prisoners. "Serious concerns remain over the capacity and commitment of these security institutions to comply with international standards," the report said.

The Conservative government tried to point out that it was the Liberals, when they had been in power, who had written the original detainee transfer agreement. That was true—at former Prime Minister Paul Martin's suggestion, then-Minister of Defence Bill Graham had concluded the original detainee transfer agreement. The agreement was supposed to ensure that any detainees Canada transferred were to be treated under the standards set out by the Third Geneva Convention. There were some initial rumblings that Hillier might have gone so far as to conclude the agreement himself, without consulting the government, but Hillier was quick to shoot those rumours down, saying he had just signed it.

Court proceedings then began to happen, too. With a growing narrative emerging that there might have been torture and abuse of detainees who had been in Canadian custody, Amnesty International Canada and the BC Civil Liberties Association launched a court challenge against the government in an effort to stop all future transfers. They were also trying to argue that, because those detainees had been in Canadian custody first, that the Charter of Rights and Freedoms should extend to them. It was this court case that would lead to several revelations as the scandal unfolded.

The first revelation came on May 3, 2007, in the form of an affidavit filed with the court for the challenge. The affidavit was from a Canadian Forces colonel by the name of Steve Noonan, who had been a task force commander in Afghanistan. In the affidavit, Noonan alleged that he saw a prisoner being abused by the Afghans, and that the prisoner had originally been taken into custody by Canadian soldiers.

"In this case, the CF learned that the detainee had been beaten by the local ANP (Afghan National Police). When we learned of this, they approached the local ANP and requested the detainee be given to them," the affidavit claimed. When the prisoner was given back to the Canadian troops, they turned him over instead to the provincial authorities in Afghanistan.

When the lawyer for Amnesty International Canada tried to find out more information about the incident in question, government lawyer J. Sanderson Graham shut down further inquiry, saying that more details might somehow jeopardize national security. Graham's claim would become a popular refrain not just in the court case, but also in the House of Commons.

That same morning, the long-awaited transfer agreement, which O'Connor originally said had been concluded when it had actually been still under negotiation, was finally approved and signed. Under the new agreement, Canadian officials now had unrestricted access to prisons in Afghanistan. They could also conduct private interviews of prisoners without Afghan jailers present. An estimate of the number of detainees who had been transferred was also floated—it estimated that roughly 40 detainees had been detained by Canadian soldiers before being transferred to Afghan authorities.

The following month, new allegations of torture became public as four detainees who had originally been captured by the Canadian Forces claimed that they were subsequently tortured by Afghan officials. The revelations were made in testimony by Peter MacKay and Stockwell Day during separate committee meetings. MacKay made it clear that Canada would investigate but that there was no physical evidence of any torture. This information was based on five visits to Afghan prisons that had taken place recently, and MacKay cited this as proof that the new transfer agreement was working.

"While these allegations are serious, it is true that the enhanced arrangement is working, that we are following up on our commitment. And that includes following up on these specific allegations with the Afghan authorities," MacKay said.

Later, in August 2007, the opposition finally got their wish when Harper shuffled his cabinet and O'Connor was moved from the Defence portfolio to National Revenue. Peter MacKay moved from Foreign Affairs to Defence, while Maxime Bernier moved to cover Foreign Affairs.

It was an auspicious move, as soon afterward, the judge overseeing the Amnesty International and BC Civil Liberties Association court case ruled that both parties could proceed with their challenge and that they could argue for a temporary injunction to prevent future transfers.

"Given that the risk of torture for transferred prisoners continues to be a very real one, we're asking the court to order that the practice of transferring prisoners cease, and that transfers should only resume if the changes necessary to diminish that risk are in place," said Alex Neve, secretary-general of Amnesty International Canada.

Amnesty International Canada soon received some additional ammunition in its court case in the form of a report from Amnesty International. The report found that torture and abuse were widespread in Afghan jails, so much so that it called on NATO to stop handing prisoners over to Afghan custody. The report specifically mentioned that detainees "have been subjected to torture and other ill treatment, including being whipped, exposed to extreme cold and deprived of food." It went on to say that Amnesty International "fears that investigations by the Canadian government into allegations may not have been 'competent' or 'impartial.'"

The report also pointed out a flaw in the Conservatives' logic—monitoring of detainees after they were transferred did nothing to actually prevent torture and abuse. It might find incidents of torture and abuse after the fact, but there was no way that monitoring could actually stop the problem.

"Monitoring is a technique to detect torture only after it happens. As such, monitoring cannot meet Canada's absolute legal obligation to prevent torture," the report read.

That report had been issued in November 2007, and by January 2008, it appeared that the concerns of Amnesty International were legitimate. The Conservative government revealed almost two months after the fact that Canada had actually put a temporary stop to all detainee transfers starting the previous November. That information was obtained in a letter filed as evidence in federal court in the case of Amnesty International Canada and the BC Civil Liberties Association against the government to halt all transfers. The letter stated:

> *As a consequence, there have been no transfers of detainees to Afghan authorities since that date. The allegation is under investigation by Afghan authorities. Canada will resume transferring detainees when it believes it can do in accordance with its legal obligations.*

While there were no specifics as to what caused the government to halt all detainee transfers, the allegations of mistreatment arose from a series of spot checks on Afghan prisons and the treatment of detainees that had been transferred to them.

Not only had the government gone two months without telling anyone that the transfers had actually been halted, but it was also still saying, when it apparently had reason enough to halt transfers, that there was no proof that any abuse had ever taken place. The Parliamentary records for that time period show that members of the opposition had asked the government several times in Question Period about the issue of detainees, but and no one ever said the transfers had been stopped. Peter MacKay had responded to one question from Liberal MP Denis Coderre by saying, "… there has not been one single, solitary, proven allegation of abuse of detainees…. Rather than producing hogwash and hornswoggle, maybe he can bring some cold, hard facts instead of this torqued rhetoric."

During arguments, government lawyer J. Sanderson Graham tried to explain that the government had debated at length whether or not to make public the fact that detainee transfers had been halted, but it eventually chose to say nothing so as not to jeopardize operational security in Afghanistan. Amnesty International lawyer Paul Champ made it clear he did not think the Conservatives made the right choice.

"They have been wrong. The consequence is people have been transferred to a real risk of torture. We can't take a chance of the generals being wrong again," Champ said.

The plot even grew to include the opposition. It was revealed later in January 2008 that both Stéphane Dion and Michael Ignatieff had been briefed on the cessation of detainee transfers when they had travelled to Afghanistan earlier. Regardless of the silence around the issue, news started to leak out of Afghanistan about what was happening to the detainees—they were now just being held by the Canadian Forces at Kandahar Airfield. When Canada took insurgents into custody, their hands and clothing were tested for explosive residue to see if they had been handling anything that could be used in the manufacture of an improvised explosive device. Once testing was completed, they could then be detained for longer, or they could be released. They were no longer transferred to the Afghan authorities.

However, although the Canadian Forces were not transferring detainees to Afghanistan, they were not stopping Afghan soldiers from detaining insurgents themselves. While on patrol in Afghanistan, Canadian soldiers were typically paired with soldiers from the Afghan National Army for training purposes. During those patrols, when they came across insurgents to take into custody, the Canadian troops would decide which prisoners they wanted to take. The Afghan soldiers, were then free to detain whomever Canada did not take. In one instance cited in the media, several insurgents were taken into custody during an operation led by the Afghan National Army but with the assistance of Canadian troops. The Afghans took four individuals from that operation into custody.

However, the cessation of transfers was enough to undermine arguments on the part of Amnesty International Canada and the BC Civil Liberties Association in their court case. Judge Anne MacTavish rejected their application to halt transfers because the transfers had already been stopped. In her ruling, she did outline several areas of concern, such as poor record keeping, the fact that some detainees seemed to have just disappeared and Afghanistan's human rights record of widespread torture and abuse. She also welcomed both parties to reapply if transfers ever resumed. That happened in February 2008, and Amnesty International Canada and the BC Civil Liberties Association quickly brought the case back to court. It was just as quickly rejected again because Judge MacTavish ruled that Afghan detainees could not seek protection under the Charter of Rights and Freedoms. Their protection, she said, fell under the Afghan constitution, international law and international humanitarian law.

The ruling was a blow to Amnesty International Canada and the BC Civil Liberties Association, but it was revealed that, during the time the transfers had been halted, the Afghan authorities had made upgrades to their detention facilities and jailers had received human rights training. One Afghan official had been fired and was in custody as a result of what had taken place.

But the hint of a cover-up was still present, and it received more fuel when it was revealed that Canada's information commissioner had sided with the

Conservatives when they had decided not to release certain documents or information about detainees on the grounds that it could have harmed relations with other countries.

"[The department] agreed to release as much information as possible while continuing to protect personal information. We supported its position to continue to withhold other information that would put the defence of Canada or Canada's allies at risk of being disclosed," said Access to Information Commissioner Robert Marleau in explaining his role. That information, paired with a revelation that Hillier had been reviewing every access to information request about the detainee issue, still looked suspicious to many observers.

Some answers on the detainee issue, however, were coming. The MPCC announced that it would hold open hearings on the subject starting in December 2008, despite assertions from the government that the MPCC was overstepping its bounds.

"I find that the threat to public confidence in the military police stemming from the allegations is real. There is a significant level of public concern with respect to these allegations," said Peter Tinsley, head of the MPCC.

Not everyone agreed that there was something that needed investigating. On October 3, the Canadian Forces National Investigative Service reported that it could not find evidence that any detainees had been mistreated. It found instances of two prisoners who had suffered injuries in Canadian custody—one of those individuals was injured when he tried to take a Canadian soldier's weapon in April 2006. The second suffered scrapes when trying to escape custody.

"The investigation was a thorough process, which included in excess of 100 interviews across Canada, the United States and the Islamic Republic of Afghanistan," said commanding officer Lieutenant-Colonel Gilles Sansterre.

That didn't stop the MPCC from opening its hearings on December 4, but it was clear from the start that the Conservative government was not going to do anything to help the commission. On the first day of hearings, Tinsey said the commission was experiencing problems getting the evidence it was asking for.

"It is clear serious challenges are being presented to the commission in terms of access to witnesses and the ongoing provision of documents. I call again on the government to cooperate on the question of witness access and document disclosure for the efficient, effective and fair process of this inquiry," Tinsey said.

The government tried to do more than just not co-operate—it actually went to court to try to have the hearings shut down. But the courts did not agree with the government and refused its request for a stay of proceedings, saying that the government had not proven why a stay was necessary. Tinsey kept fighting for access, grinding on until October 2009, when he again made it clear what kind of obstruction he was up against. The Conservatives had refused to reappoint him to his position and actually hadn't appointed anyone. They had imposed national security restrictions on what witnesses could say at the inquiry and what evidence could be submitted. Although Tinsey had the proper security clearance to view confidential material, the government refused to grant him the ability to examine such material "in camera," or in private.

And more bombshell revelations were coming from the MPCC, and the biggest exploded on October 14, 2009. On that date, the commission received an affidavit from Richard Colvin, a career diplomat who had spent 18 months serving in Afghanistan. In his affidavit, Colvin stated that soon after he landed in Afghanistan, he became aware of allegations of abuse and torture of prisoners. Furthermore, he went on to say that he had authored several reports that were sent back to Canada in which he warned that torture and abuse were likely taking place. He stated that his first report had been sent to Canada in April 2006, yet one year later, the government was still saying publicly that there were no credible reports of abuse.

"I spent considerable time on the detainee file and sent many reports on detainee-related issues to Canadian officials," Colvin wrote in his affidavit.

The government had actually tried to stop Colvin and 21 others from testifying at the MPCC hearings by arguing that Colvin and the rest had nothing relevant to offer and that they might inadvertently disclose sensitive information. In the end, the Conservatives got their wish. Shortly after Colvin's affidavit was released, Peter Tinsey announced that the inquiry was shutting down because of lack of support from the Conservative government. Specifically, the government refused to hand over documents that might help one implicated member of the military police to craft a defence.

"This is how we find ourselves where we are today, forced to adjourn the proceedings out of fairness to the subjects since obviously they should not be the ones to suffer because of the government's conduct," Tinsey said.

But Colvin's claim that he had authored numerous reports that warned of torture and abuse reverberated through Ottawa. Both Gordon O'Connor and Peter MacKay claimed that they had never heard of Colvin's reports. That looked particularly bad for MacKay, as he had been Colvin's boss as Minister of Foreign Affairs at the time the reports were written. New Chief of the Defence Staff Walter Natynczyk announced that he would look for Colvin's reports to see what happened to them after they were sent. Former chief Rick Hillier, when contacted, stated that he did not remember reading Colvin's reports.

Hillier had just published his memoirs, *A Soldier First*. In his book, Hillier wrote that the government likely knew of military intelligence stating that detainees were being abused. In his book, he wrote:

> *The previous fall (2007), we had told Foreign Affairs, CIDA and the rest of the government that, unless inspectors visited Afghan jails continually and built confidence that those detained by us were still being treated humanely, we were not going to transfer any more. We had made sure everyone knew that we were stopping those transfers.*

Colvin's testimony was now seen as important, and though the MPCC had been shut down, a House of Commons committee on Afghanistan was holding hearings into the detainee issue, and Colvin was called to testify. At the hearing, Colvin made a few stunning claims. He said that he was told by David Mulroney, once the prime minister's national security advisor, to report what he found only by phone and to not put anything in writing. He also claimed that Hillier was well aware that detainees were being abused. That abuse, he said, consisted of detainees being beaten with power cables, given electric shocks and deprived of sleep.

"According to our information, the likelihood is that all the Afghans we handed over were tortured," Colvin told the committee.

The Conservatives responded by trying to shred Colvin's reputation. First came Peter MacKay, who replied, when questioned in the House of Commons about Colvin's testimony, that Colvin's evidence was hearsay and might as well have come from the Taliban. He went so far as to claim that Colvin's story was full of holes, but then went on to say that it was because of Colvin's reports that the new transfer agreement had been signed—a contradiction that the opposition pounced on.

It was through these committee hearings that it came to light that the government had again halted all transfers, not just once, but three times in 2009 over fears of mistreatment of detainees. Based on this information and Colvin's testimony, the opposition started to ask for a public inquiry into the detainee issue.

"What the government is apparently doing now is they're dribbling out little bits and pieces of information," said NDP leader Jack Layton. "This underlies the importance of having a full inquiry as we proposed. Let's have a proper investigation to get to the bottom of it because otherwise there's this attitude developing globally…that maybe the Canadian government is covering up when it comes to the issue of human rights and torture, and that's not acceptable."

The government continued to attack Colvin's testimony and his reputation. It produced three generals for the next committee hearing, including Rick Hillier, but also Lieutenant-General Michael Gauthier and Major General David Fraser, all of whom testified before the committee that they never received any warnings or read any reports by Colvin about torture. Hillier said he had even reread all of Colvin's reports and found no references to abuse. When Peter MacKay and Gordon O'Connor later testified before the committee, they also claimed they had never been told of or read any report about abuse. In response to all the criticism, Colvin responded with a 16-page rebuttal, claiming that the government had ignored his reports, censored the content and was now trying to smear him and his testimony.

But stories were emerging. In one case, Natynczyk had testified about an incident in which a solider taken into custody by Canadian soldiers and then transferred was later found being beaten by Afghan police officers, using their shoes. The troops took that detainee away immediately for medical attention. When Natynczyk first recounted that episode, he had claimed the insurgent had not first been in Canadian custody. He was later forced to correct himself when he learned that Canadian soldiers had the insurgent in custody to begin with.

The opposition was starting to press the government for more information, going so far as to put a motion before the House of Commons calling on the government to provide unedited documentation that related to the detainee affair. And the motion actually passed, 145–143. But the Conservative government refused to obey the motion, which created a new conflict. An argument now developed over what branch of the government was the most powerful—the legislative branch—Parliament—or the executive branch—cabinet.

Rather than continue to face an increasing number of questions from the opposition over the growing detainee scandal, Stephen Harper decided it was time to take a break. On December 30, 2009, Harper called the Governor General and prorogued Parliament for two months. While he said publicly that it was because the Olympics were coming to Vancouver in February, it was widely seen as a move to avoid continued pressure and embarrassment on the detainee file. It did not go unnoticed that, with the prorogation of Parliament, all of the House committees, including the committee investigating the detainee issue, were shut down.

"This is beyond arrogant," said Liberal Ralph Goodale, the party house leader. "It really does border upon despotic behaviour. The only objective here is to muzzle Parliament."

"The decision to prorogue is about one thing and one thing only—avoiding the scrutiny of Parliament at a time when this government is facing tough questions about their conduct in covering up the detainee scandal," Liberal Michael Ignatieff said.

The Conservatives tried to quell the ongoing rumblings over the decision to prorogue by claiming that the committee would be reconstituted once Parliament returned. The Conservatives had also asked former Supreme Court Justice Frank Iacobucci to examine documents pertaining to the detainee scandal to determine which ones could be released. But all that ignored what was quickly becoming the central issue—that Stephen Harper's government was ignoring a motion by the House of Commons calling on his government to release unedited documentation on the detainee issue.

The opposition brought that issue back to the House of Commons when it returned from its impromptu break. In March 2010, the opposition parties united to call on the government to honour the December vote or face being found in contempt of Parliament. Speaker Peter Milliken was asked to rule on the question of who was in the right—Parliament or the Conservative government.

On April 27, Milliken handed down his ruling in favour of Parliament.

"It is the view of the chair that accepting an unconditional authority of the executive to censor the information provided to Parliament would, in fact, jeopardize the very separation of powers that is purported to lie at the heart of our parliamentary system and the independence of its constituent parts," Milliken said. "Furthermore, it risks diminishing the inherent privileges of the House and its members, which have been earned and must be safeguarded."

More simply stated, Milliken found that the Conservatives, in refusing to obey the December 10 motion to produce documents, had breached parliamentary privilege.

Surprisingly, the Conservatives acquiesced to Milliken's ruling and were able to craft a compromise of sorts with the opposition. An ad hoc committee was formed of Conservative, Liberal and Bloc Québécois MPs, all of whom were granted access to the estimated 40,000 documents pertaining to the detainee file. A panel of three judges was also appointed to help them determine which documents should be made public and which should not. They did agree on a list of items that would remain confidential, and those included cabinet confidences, as well as any documents in which government or officials made negative remarks about the Afghan people or institutions. Communications between foreign governments, the ICRC and NATO were also to remain confidential and would be redacted.

And the Conservatives did more. In September 2010, after years of maintaining that the exact number of detainees transferred to Afghan custody was a matter of national security, it finally served up a statistic for the public to digest. Between 2001 and 2008, the Canadian Forces had taken 439 prisoners. Of that total, 283 were transferred to Afghan custody—more than 50 percent of the total number of detainees taken into custody by Canadian soldiers. There were no numbers given, however, with respect to how many of that 283 were alleged to have been abused or tortured by the Afghan authorities once they were transferred into their custody.

Despite the Conservatives' sudden willingness to cooperate and make information public, this was not the beginning of a renaissance of openness for the party. In April 2011, it emerged that the government was in court, trying to once again limit the work of the MPCC. Although the commission had halted its hearings, it was still trying to issue a report. The government was trying to stop it from including evidence from key witnesses such as Richard Colvin.

Less than one year later, the Conservatives suddenly made public 4000 pages of documents on the detainee file. The government maintained that these documents it had finally released proved that Canada never knew before detainees were handed over to the Afghan authorities whether or not they could face torture. Stéphane Dion, who was one of the Liberals selected to go through the documents produced by the Conservatives, begged to differ, telling reporters there was a greater likelihood that those taken into custody and transferred had been tortured. He said that while Canadian troops acted professionally, the government had failed to accurately track the detainees it was transferring, and what inspections were done, were often inadequate and were conducted erratically.

"[The inspections] were not sufficient to really protect these hundreds of people," Dion said.

The release of documents, and the end of Canada's combat mission in Afghanistan, effectively brought the detainee matter to a quiet end. It had taken years of work and pressure, but the Conservatives had finally made public some of the information that so many had been asking about for years.

CHAPTER FOUR

Maxime Bernier Affair

RELATIONSHIPS IN THE fishbowl that is Ottawa and Parliament Hill can be tricky. And though it appears that Maxime Bernier could appreciate those difficulties, the Conservative member of Parliament demonstrated that, no matter what kind of conditions you place on a romantic relationship, you can't control for every possible outcome, especially when it comes to your own mistakes.

Bernier, representing the constituency of Beauce, was something of a rising star when he decided to stand as a candidate in the 2006 federal election. Of course, when it came to the Conservatives and their status in Québec at the time of the election, it didn't take much beyond a little name recognition to qualify as a star candidate. In the 2004 election, the Conservatives had been entirely shut out, not electing a single MP in the province.

Bernier, though, came from a Conservative Québec lineage—his own father had represented Beauce in Ottawa, first as a Progressive Conservative, and then as an Independent, so the Bernier name was well-known in the area. A lawyer by education, Bernier had worked predominately in banking and finance. Before putting his name forward as the Conservative candidate for Beauce, he was a vice-president of the Standard Life of Canada insurance company. In the 2006 election, he sailed to victory, capturing more than 36,000 votes, while the second-place finisher managed only 10,997 votes.

Given his star power in Québec, his youth (he was 46 when elected) and his experience in finance and banking, he was quickly named to cabinet as Minister of Industry, where he stayed until the summer of 2007, when he was tapped as the next Minister of Foreign Affairs for Canada. From the day he was sworn in as Minister of Foreign Affairs, Bernier's time in the position was filled with a level of bumbling drama that few could have predicted.

Whenever a cabinet is sworn in by the Governor General, the appointees assemble at Rideau Hall for the occasion. It's a pretty big deal to be named to cabinet, and many of those who are selected bring their spouses or family members to attend the usually brief ceremony. Bernier was no exception—he decided to bring his girlfriend, a realtor by the name of Julie Couillard, whom he had been dating for a few months. As the two walked up toward Rideau Hall, holding hands, all eyes—and camera lenses—turned to take in what Couillard was wearing. It was a dress, but *what* a dress! It was brown and blue and paisley-patterned, with a halter neck whose plunging neckline made a great deal of Couillard's cleavage visible to everyone. The wardrobe choice was criticized heavily, considering the occasion for which the dress was worn. It was even later revealed that the Prime Minister's Office had talked to Bernier about Couillard's dress, which was believed to have been too revealing.

The fuss over the dress almost proved to be an omen, but not only with respect to Couillard and Bernier's relationship—it was as if the minor controversy over the dress sent Bernier down the wrong path as Minister of Foreign Affairs. In October 2007, just a few months after being sworn in, Bernier made a trip to Afghanistan to visit Canadian troops, specifically members of the Van Doos, or the Royal 22nd Regiment, who were fighting in the ongoing war in that country. Bernier had decided in advance of the trip that he wanted to bring something to the troops as a gesture, and snack cakes came to mind, specifically Jos. Louis snack cakes, which had been created in Bernier's home constituency of Beauce. What followed was a shopping spree by members of the Canadian Forces in Canada, who had to desperately try to acquire the approximately 2000 snack cakes needed for Bernier's trip, even though they had been given less than 24 hours to get that many of the treats together. In the end, after raiding stores throughout Ontario, the soldiers managed to collect approximately 2100 Jos. Louis snack cakes for the trip overseas.

Unfortunately, the image of the Minister of Foreign Affairs rewarding Canadian soldiers serving in a war with a treat did not go over well back home in Canada.

"We thank our soldiers for their work and their sacrifice by giving them treats," said Liberal MP Denis Coderre. "That's nice."

Afghanistan would actually prove to be difficult territory for Bernier. In April 2008, he made a very public, very international gaffe during another visit to the war-torn country. He was making some remarks to reporters gathered at Kandahar Airfield when the question of corruption in Afghanistan and, specifically, what more President Hamid Karzai could do about corruption around Kandahar, came up.

Bernier replied, "As you know, there is always the question of the governor here. I think [Mr. Karzai] can work with us to be sure the governor will be more powerful; the governor will do what he has to do to help us. There's a question to maybe have a new governor. Is the right person at the right place at the right time? President Karzai will have to answer those questions as soon as possible."

To the reporters gathered around, it sounded like Bernier had just said that the current governor of Kandahar province—Asadullah Khalid—was corrupt and needed replacing. His remarks were seen as interfering in the internal affairs of a sovereign nation, something that is considered a diplomatic no-no in the world of foreign affairs. Within hours, Bernier was forced to issue a statement retracting and clarifying what he had said:

> *Afghanistan is a sovereign state that makes its own decisions about government appointments. I can assure you that Canada fully respects this and is not calling for any changes to the Afghan government. In fact, our primary goal is promoting the self-sufficiency of Afghanistan in all aspects of nationhood, including development, security and governance. We will continue working closely with all levels of the Afghan government to advance this objective.*

Bernier's remarks quickly made their way back to Canada, where Peter Van Loan, the Conservative House leader, was forced to respond to questions from the opposition that "the affairs of the Afghan government are the affairs of the Afghan government. It is a sovereign country, and it is responsible for its own nominations and its own appointments. We do not make those decisions for the people of Kandahar."

Even Prime Minister Stephen Harper, who was in Winnipeg at the time, was forced to admit that Bernier's statements had led to some "misimpressions."

It appeared that the month of May might give Bernier a bit of relief. On May 1, Bernier was named the sexiest male MP in the House of Commons by the *Hill Times*, unseating fellow Conservative Peter MacKay. He also defeated Liberal MP Scott Brison as best-dressed male MP. The results were based on a survey of Parliamentary staff. Kate Malloy, editor of the *Hill Times*, let it be known that the choice was reflective not just of Bernier's appearance, but also of the look of his girlfriend, Julie Couillard.

"Maxime Bernier's date helped," Malloy was quoted as saying.

But the reprieve didn't last. Too soon after that dubious honour, Bernier was in the spotlight again with respect to an international issue.

On May 2, 2008, Cyclone Nargis slammed into Myanmar, formerly known as Burma. Packing winds that reached speeds of 215 kilometres per hour, the Category 4 tropical cyclone devastated the isolated Asian country, killing an estimated 138,000 people and causing an estimated US$10 billion in damages. It was the worst natural disaster in the country's recorded history, and the entire world quickly stepped up with offers of assistance. Yet that help was not accepted at first because Myanmar was ruled by a military junta that was reluctant to allow outsiders within its borders. Aid workers for agencies ready to provide help to the millions of affected people of Myanmar had to spend several days in Thailand because the military junta refused to issue them visas. On May 6, the country's representative to the United Nations officially requested help, and aid started to trickle into the country shortly afterward.

Canada promptly announced $2 million in aid, which was quickly criticized by the opposition as a paltry amount given the scope of rebuilding that Myanmar was facing. But Bernier further complicated the situation two weeks later, even though he was, it seems, trying to help. Bernier had met in Rome with the director of the World Food Program (WFP). The military junta in Myanmar had authorized the WFP to bring 10 of its helicopters to Myanmar to help with the aid efforts, and the WFP was looking for a way of getting the helicopters to the country rapidly. Bernier was quick to offer Canada's assistance.

"Canada is there to help the people of Burma, and we have a C-17 available," Bernier was quoted as saying after the meeting, referring to the C-17 Globemaster II transport planes. "We'll do this flight as quickly as possible."

At first glance, Bernier had made a sensible offer. Canada had just recently purchased four of the cavernous transport Globemasters, receiving the first one only a year prior. The behemoth aircraft were capable of carrying payloads of up to 77,500 kilograms for a distance of up to 4400 kilometres without needing to stop for fuel.

But Bernier was missing an important piece of information—none of Canada's four C-17s were actually available to take the WFP's helicopters anywhere. Two of the planes were on scheduled assignments, while the other two were undergoing repairs and maintenance. Faced with a promise it did not have the resources to actually carry out, the government was forced to take the expensive step of renting a transport aircraft to fulfil Bernier's pledge. It was not an uncommon step for Canada to take—it had, for years, rented airlift planes to fulfil its strategic airlift needs. But one of the reasons the Conservatives had purchased the C-17s in the first place, at a cost of $3.4 billion, was to put a stop to the practice. But with Bernier having pledged the military's support to the WFP, the government had no choice but to rent a Russian Antonov transport plane to move the helicopters—at a cost of $900,000.

"The transportation of helicopters on behalf of the World Food Program is an urgent mission. In order to alleviate human suffering as quickly as possible, a commercially chartered aircraft will be used to fly four helicopters from Ukraine to Thailand simultaneously," one of Bernier's spokespeople was quoted as saying.

The criticism from the opposition was swift.

"It seems incredible the Harper government purchased these heavy-lift aircraft and told us at the time we'd no longer have to [rent] planes and now we're going to spend another $900,000 to ship aid to Burma," said NDP defence critic Dawn Black.

Bernier's original promise might not have been possible even if the C-17s had been available, it was later revealed. The consensus was that the helicopters would have needed to be taken apart to fit in the plane, then reassembled once in country.

It was an embarrassing situation for the Tories and for Bernier, but if he was making mistakes, perhaps it was because he was distracted. A bombshell had been dropped earlier in the month that was echoing throughout Ottawa and the entire nation, and it centred on Bernier's romantic life.

This particular controversy had nothing to do with the fashion taste of Julie Couillard. The problem was the men she had been involved with prior to meeting Bernier. Reports stated that Couillard had had relationships with men who were linked to the biker gangs of Québec.

It was a hair-raising revelation that reverberated not just in Québec, but in official Ottawa as well. The Québec biker gangs were not simply social clubs of like-minded motorcycle enthusiasts. They were criminals, and the ongoing conflict between different gangs trying to control narcotics distribution throughout the province of Québec was deadly. There had even been a period of history, from 1994 to 2002, that was referred to as "Québec's biker war," in which the Hells Angels and Rock Machine gangs had battled for control of the drug trade. One hundred and fifty people were killed during the war in waves of bombings and retaliatory murders.

Specifically, the initial reports on Couillard stated that she had been married to a Québec bike gang member. Experts contacted by the media seemed to agree that Bernier's affiliation with Couillard, given the new information, could pose a risk to security, given the sensitive information that Bernier handled on a regular basis.

The possibility that a minister of the Crown had been romantically involved with a woman with links to an organized crime group brought immediate condemnation from the opposition. At first, the Conservatives feigned indignation that the opposition was intruding into the private life of one of its ministers.

"I hear that one of my cabinet ministers has an ex-girlfriend. It's none of my business. It's none of Mr. Duceppe's business. It's none of Mr. Dion's business," Harper said, referring to the leaders of two of the opposition parties. "Mr. Duceppe and Mr. Dion are quite a group of gossipy old busybodies."

Couillard and Bernier were, at first, unwilling to discuss the subject.

When contacted by phone, all Couillard would say was, "The record will be set straight, but not right now," before hanging up.

Bernier said, "This is about my private life, the private life in the past of my ex-girlfriend. People's private lives are none of the members' business."

The opposition quickly started asking if Couillard had ever been the subject of a security check since she had begun dating Bernier. The Privy Council Office, which is responsible for the federal government's bureaucracy, replied that it conducts background checks on candidates for cabinet posts, but not on their family, friends or significant others. A quick check, however, revealed that Couillard did not have a criminal record.

But as the press started digging into Couillard's past, they turned up more information into her biker ties that revealed she had not been involved with just one man who was linked to Québec's biker gangs—there had been at least two men with links to the criminal underworld.

One of those men, Stéphane Sirois, was a biker to whom Couillard had been married. Sirois had been a member of the Rockers, a puppet club of the Hells Angels. According to testimony at the 2003 murder trial of Hells Angels leader Maurice "Mom" Boucher, Sirois had testified that the Hells Angels didn't trust Couillard and had made him choose between her and the club. Sirois had testified at the trial as an informant. He was later placed in a witness-protection program and given a new identity.

Before Sirois, Couillard had been in a relationship with Gilles Giguère, who had been linked to the Hells Angels. Giguère and two other Hells Angels had been charged with extortion, and Couillard had even been arrested in a raid involving Giguère, but she was not charged and was released after questioning. Giguère was found shot to death after his arrest.

A picture of Couillard and her behaviour in her time with Bernier was also starting to emerge. It was revealed that Couillard had started asking to sit in on Bernier's media interviews. She had even sought access to some of the confidential meetings he had attended, but she had been turned down by authorities. And Bernier and Couillard were seen together around Ottawa months after his communication staff had said the pair had broken up.

On May 26, 2008, Bernier officially resigned as Minister of Foreign Affairs. The move was announced by Prime Minister Stephen Harper. David Emmerson, serving as Minister of International Trade, took over Bernier's portfolio.

Harper announced that Bernier had decided to resign after he realized he had left secure documents in an unsecure area. He did not, however, reveal anything about the documents or their contents, or where they might have been left and who might have seen them. He also said the resignation had nothing to do with Julie Couillard.

"This is a grave mistake. We're always expecting from the ministers to keep secret, classified documents, government documents. This [has nothing] to do with the minister's private life. I'm very disappointed," Harper said. "I'm very disappointed for the government, disappointed for Maxime. It is very unfortunate."

There was immediate speculation that Couillard herself was going to appear on television that evening. And it was true—Couillard did give an interview to Québec television station TVA. In the interview, she said she believed someone had been watching her since the scandal broke. She went on to claim that a team of security experts had searched her home since the news first broke of her biker ties. Those experts claimed to have found signs that a microphone had likely been planted in the box spring of her mattress. She also claimed that she had been up front with Bernier about her romantic past.

"Maxime knew about it," she said.

Couillard also revealed that, contrary to what Harper had said earlier in the day, she was involved in Bernier's resignation from cabinet. The insecure place in which Bernier had left confidential documents was, in fact, her home. Couillard said he had left the documents behind at some point in the previous month. She had talked with her lawyer, who advised her to give the documents back to the government.

Couillard told the interviewer that it was Bernier who told her to wear the infamous dress to Rideau Hall the previous summer. She also provided a bit of background on her biker ties, saying that Giguère, who it turned out had been gunned down after he had decided to become a police informant, was not a biker and was merely a friend of someone who knew Hells Angels leader Maurice Boucher. She had lived with Giguère from 1993 to 1996. She had started dating Sirois in 1997 and married him, but divorced him in 1999.

The news about Couillard didn't stop there. Shortly after the interview was broadcast, it was revealed that she had been part of a bid for a security contract at Trudeau International Airport. The bid had been made in 2004 and had been unsuccessful. The name of the company that made the bid and with which Couillard had been involved was Agence d'investigations et de sécurité DRP. As part of the bid, Couillard and her then-boyfriend, Robert Pépin, had access to information about security arrangements at the airport.

Pépin and Couillard split up in 2005. He had allegedly owed a lot of money to a Hells Angels loan shark and had started receiving threats as a result of the debt. He later committed suicide.

Liberal leader Michael Ignatieff was critical.

"This is about the possibility...of a link between organized crime and airport security in Montréal and the possibility of improper bidding for contracts relating to security."

And the opposition was also howling for more information about what had happened with the documents left at Couillard's home, even suggesting that a probe might be necessary to get to the bottom of the story. It came out that the documents had actually been missing for several weeks. Government House leader Peter Van Loan confirmed that the documents in question were actually a mixture of both classified and unclassified material relating to a NATO summit that had been held in Romania the previous month. They had been missing for a total of five weeks.

That fact was perplexing to those who know how classified and secure documents are handled in Ottawa. For a document to go missing for five weeks with apparently no one noticing seemed strange. Previous cabinet ministers had said that all confidential documents were checked out and then checked back in. Any missing documents were located as quickly as possible. Cabinet ministers typically had safes installed in their homes in which they were supposed to keep confidential documents when they took them home.

It also emerged that Couillard was trying to get paid for her interviews—she had apparently been shopping her exclusive story to the media, asking for $50,000 for an interview. She was a registered real estate agent, but no one could find any record that she had ever worked at the agency under which she was registered. She had also been an executive of a security company called Itek Solutions—a group that had biker gang links.

On May 29, the Liberals decided to add to the heat already on Bernier and the Conservatives. MP and former BC premier Ujjal Dosanjh suggested that sometime between May 1 and May 8, CSIS had met with the Prime Minister's Office to discuss Bernier's situation. The Conservatives dismissed Dosanjh's story as "wild," but Dosanjh stuck to his guns, refusing to reveal the source of the story but insisting that his source was credible. The Liberals also asked the RCMP to step in and investigate. An Ipsos poll found that a slim majority of Canadians (55 percent) agreed that the Mounties should take a closer look. Thirty-nine percent of those polled insisted that a more thorough investigation was necessary.

Later that day, Bernier finally issued an apology.

"With humility, I take full and sole responsibility for my actions. I also express regret over the negative impact caused by my recent events on Ms. Couillard's private life. Furthermore, I refuse to discuss private affairs in a public forum."

Couillard was still talking to the media. On May 29, the magazine 7 *Jours* published an interview with her in which she revealed that she believed Bernier never actually loved her. She was highly critical of him.

"I saw him as a much different man than he was in reality. What disappointed me was that he didn't have the backbone that I believed he had."

Couillard also revealed that the documents had been left at her home for a period of five weeks, and in that time, Bernier had not once contacted her about trying to get them back.

On June 3, the House Standing Committee on Public Safety and National Security announced that it would begin hearings on June 10 into the Bernier affair. It also announced that it would ask the prime minister to testify as part of its investigation. Given that the majority of the seats on the committee were filled by opposition members, it came as no surprise the following day when it was announced that no Conservative MPs, including the prime minister, would be appearing before the committee.

There were more revelations to come about Couillard's relationships. It was revealed in June 2008 that, in the early 1990s, she had been romantically linked to a man named Tony Volpato, who was a close friend of Mafia leader Frank Cotroni. At the time Couillard and Volpato were together, Volpato was under investigation for cigarette smuggling involving the Kahnawake Indian Reserve. He was found guilty in 1997 and fined $8000. That same year, he was sentenced to six years in prison for his role in a conspiracy to import 180 kilograms of cocaine.

On the second day of hearings, the RCMP appeared before the Standing Committee on Public Safety and National Security. The RCMP said that they perform background checks on certain office holders, but that doesn't extend to spouses or romantic partners. In the case of security clearances, the RCMP said those people can be interviewed, but the force didn't conduct security clearances. They also stated without going into any real detail that Couillard was a "known" person.

The government announced an investigation into the affair, but it was being handled in-house by Foreign Affairs and was widely seen as a Conservative attempt to whitewash whatever had happened. Bernier stated that he would participate in the investigation. Shortly after his announcement, however, the affair grew increasingly complex when it was revealed that Bernard Côté, an advisor to Public Works Minister Michael Fortier, had been ordered to resign after it was discovered by a Montréal tabloid that he, too, had dated Couillard.

Specifically, he was forced to resign because he did not reveal his relationship with her, and he did not step away from handling a file with which she was also involved. The two had been dating at the same time as a company with which she was associated—Kevlar Group—was seeking a government contract. Kevlar Group, a real estate company, had been bidding for a massive Québec City building project. Kevlar Group initially responded by denying that Couillard was an employee, then later admitted she was on the company's payroll.

Everyone was waiting to hear more from Couillard, but they would have to wait. She declined a June 16 invitation to testify before the Standing Committee on Public Safety and National Security, saying in a letter written by her lawyer that she could face charges under the Security of Information Act. Testifying before the committee, especially after it was revealed that Maxime Bernier wasn't going to be testifying, would put her at further risk of being prosecuted.

"If the committee wishes my client to publicly disclose all the circumstances surrounding the secret documents having been 'left' at her residence by an inattentive minister, her fundamental right to make a full and complete defence could be seriously affected in a subsequent trial," the letter said.

The letter also stated that Couillard believed the RCMP might be investigating her.

Whatever the committee was hoping to hear, it was soon revealed that they and every other Canadian would get the chance to find out more in the fall. On June 21, Couillard announced that she would be publishing her autobiography.

With the exception of issuing one formal apology after his resignation, Bernier had stayed quiet since he had resigned. He actually spent some time at a monastery after his resignation in order to contemplate his future. That changed on June 26 when, during a speech in his constituency, Bernier said that he didn't know anything about Couillard's past until the two of them had stopped seeing each other.

"She did not inform me and never has anyone else at any level. I knew of her past what she would tell me and was only told rumours concerning her past on April 20, a few weeks before the information became public, and at the time we were no longer dating."

He also explained why the documents he had left at her place had gone unnoticed in Ottawa for so long.

"The briefing notes were not sensitive enough to be barcoded, so they did not set off any alarms," he said.

On August 2, the government released its findings into the scandal. It did so in a way that infuriated reporters—as part of a document dump on the evening of the Friday before a long weekend. When reporters had time to digest the review, they read that the government had not found that Bernier had caused "significant injury to the national interest" by leaving documents at Couillard's house. They also stated that this was a one-time occurrence and was not a symptom of a larger problem with respect to handling documents. The report did concede that, given the nature of the documents at issue, the incident might have impacted "Canada's good reputation within NATO circles for safeguarding classified information."

The furor over the affair died down until October, when Couillard's much-anticipated autobiography, *My Story*, was released. In the book, Couillard described what led to the documents being left at her house. She wrote that Bernier had stayed the night, and in the morning, April 19, as he was getting ready to leave, he had dumped a stack of papers on the kitchen counter of her home in Laval and then asked her to put them in the garbage.

"The next garbage pickup wasn't until the following Friday. In the meantime, other papers piled up on top of them, and I forgot all about them. But I was soon to be reminded of their existence in quite brutal fashion," she wrote.

There were other revelations in the book, and none of them made Bernier look good. Couillard wrote that when the pair had started dating, Bernier had put a condition on their relationship that it would be for at least one year. Even if they were to end their relationship before the one-year mark, they had to keep making appearances together. Bernier had told her that was because as a cabinet minister, he could not give the appearance that he was dating woman after woman. She also wrote that, in dating her, he was trying to put an end to rumours that he was gay. The pair had broken up in December, she revealed, but kept up appearances together afterward as he had requested. She wrote of his constant complaining and criticisms of Prime Minister Stephen Harper and claimed that Bernier was very vain, superficial "and displayed a surprising degree of intellectual laziness."

"All in all, Maxime was quite full of himself and extremely superficial. He didn't seem particularly conscious of his responsibilities, and I never saw him deeply absorbed in his dossiers. He wasn't interested in such things; in fact, I think that apathy in large part explains the gaffes he committed during his time as Minister of Foreign Affairs," Couillard wrote.

Bernier was quick to reply to the book.

"She is frustrated and wants to have glory. She wants to have visibility, and she is using every means to do it. I made an error in going out with that woman, but that is in the past and I have turned toward the future," he said.

In April 2009, the dress that had launched Bernier's problems made a brief comeback when Couillard put it up for sale as part of a fundraiser for pediatric epilepsy. A Montréal gynecologist purchased it for $1000.

"What happened with this dress is just living proof of the fact that sexism is still out there," Couillard was quoted as saying about the dress.

In September 2009, more than a year after the scandal first broke, the government finally made available heavily redacted copies of the documents Bernier had left at Couillard's house. The topics in the documents ranged from climate change to concerns about Russia and the Middle East, missile defence, troop deployments in Afghanistan, NATO enlargement and the al-Qaeda threat in Afghanistan. Opposition critics said that the heavy redaction of the documents was proof that they were more sensitive than the government had initially claimed, but the furor had died down. The scandal was over.

Bernier spent another four years in the backbenches before getting his second chance. In July 2013, Bernier was re-appointed to cabinet, this time as the Minister of State (Small Business, Tourism and Agriculture).

CHAPTER FIVE

2008 Prorogation of Parliament

THE WANING MONTHS OF 2008 featured a convergence of events that Canadians might never see—thankfully—align in history ever again. The beginnings of a recession, a federal election and a constitutional crisis all emerged, and given our increasingly digital age, Canadians were able to follow all three in almost real-time as the world teetered on the brink of a global financial crisis that threatened much of the economic growth of the last decade. Yet while such an event should have spurred Canada's government to consider how it could best protect its citizens from the effects of a recession, we were instead witnesses to the kind of fierce partisanship—predominately from the Conservatives—that, in the end, benefits no one. It created a one-of-a-kind crisis that we can only hope will never happen again.

But I will say this—as a former journalist, the events of November and December 2008 were riveting and fascinating to watch.

Before Stephen Harper launched his misguided attempt to destroy the other political parties in Ottawa, the world's economic system was teetering on the brink of collapse, courtesy of the United States. The narrative of late 2008 typically plays out like this—housing prices in the United States started to fall dramatically as the housing bubble began to burst. In the hot economy that had preceded the crisis, many financial institutions had engaged in risky behaviour, predominately in extending subprime mortgages to candidates who, under normal circumstances, would not have been granted credit. Those individuals, having taken on a substantial amount of household debt, found themselves unable to repay their mortgages and subsequently defaulted. Financial institutions were then left with large numbers of defaulted mortgages for homes that were worth far less than what they had been when the mortgage was issued. Furthermore, financial institutions had used those same mortgages as securities, meaning that when the homeowners defaulted, the security defaulted as well.

Homeowners were also using those mortgages to refinance debt and then spending that money on other goods, as opposed to investing in savings. Soon the banking industry was in trouble, the depth of its difficulties symbolized by the total failure of the Lehman Brothers bank in September 2008, and other institutions started going bankrupt or seeking financial assistance. The effects of the subprime mortgage crisis quickly extended into the rest of the economy. As business and consumer confidence plunged, financial firms stopped investing altogether in households because they were facing budget crunches of their own and possible loss of employment, so they stopped spending. Soon credit was being withdrawn, investments were stopped and economic growth came to screeching halt.

It was under these conditions, as the economic picture became ever darker and one week before the titanic bankruptcy of Lehman Brothers, that Stephen Harper asked Governor General Michaëlle Jean to dissolve Parliament and send Canadians back to the polls. The decision to seek an election was something of a scandal in and of itself—the previous Parliament had passed the Conservatives' amendment to the Canada Elections Act that provided for a fixed election date. The next election was not supposed to take place until October 2009. Harper claimed that Parliament had grown dysfunctional—the Conservatives had withstood several confidence motions and had, in fact, managed to put together the longest minority government in Canada's history, lasting from April 3, 2006, to September 7, 2008. At the time of the dissolution of the House of Commons, the Conservatives held 124 seats, the Liberals 103, the Bloc Québécois 51 and the NDP 29. There was also one Independent member of Parliament.

In the upcoming election, scheduled to take place on October 14, Harper had one new adversary—new Liberal leader Stéphane Dion. He was also up against Bloc leader Gilles Duceppe and NDP leader Jack Layton. With the global economic picture growing increasingly stark, the campaign centred on the economy. Harper found himself insisting that, regardless of the global financial picture, he would not return Canada to a deficit position.

The results that came in on October 14 gave Harper's Conservatives a slightly larger minority government, but not the majority he had been hoping for. At the end of the night, the Conservatives held 143 seats, the Liberals had dropped to 77, the Bloc held 49 and the NDP had 37, with two Independent MPs elected. Following the election, Liberal leader Stéphane Dion announced that he would resign as leader of the party in May 2009, giving the Liberals time to hold a new leadership race.

As Stephen Harper prepared for the Speech from the Throne following his election win, he made it clear that the changing financial crisis gripping the entire globe might require a change in thinking by his party. Specifically, although on the campaign trail he had said he would never put Canada back into deficit, Harper was now less certain.

"We put a high value on keeping the budget balanced, but the truth of the matter is we are less certain about the future today than we were even a few weeks ago," Harper was quoted as saying in one interview, indicating that his stance toward deficit spending was starting to soften.

The Speech from the Throne that followed in November 2008 was much more sombre and glum than the usual such speech. Typically, a Speech from the Throne is big on words and sparse with details on what is actually going to happen. But the speech, as read by Governor General Michaëlle Jean, sought to warn Canadians that tough times were ahead.

"In a historic global downturn, it would be misguided to commit to a balanced budget in the short term at any cost because the cost would ultimately be borne by Canadian families," Jean said. The speech also referred to a close examination of government spending. There were hints of other actions as well, such as freezing the salaries of civil servants and reducing spending on grants, contributions and capital expenditures.

The financial news continued to grow increasingly dire. Parliamentary Budget Officer Kevin Page issued a report shortly after the Speech from the Throne, giving a range of possible budget outcomes for the federal government. His worst-case scenario predicted a $14 billion deficit as likely for 2009—a massive shift from the originally predicted $2.3 billion surplus for 2008 and $1.3 billion for 2009. More "average" forecasts called for deficits of between $1.7 billion and $6 billion in the following year. Page's report came on the heels of an announcement that in a week's time, Finance Minister Jim Flaherty would give a fiscal update to the House of Commons.

As happens with any major announcement, news of what would be contained in the fiscal update leaked out in advance of its presentation in the House of Commons, and the response from the opposition parties was ferocious. There would be a clamp down on spending at the government level—salaries of politicians and senior civil servants would be frozen, and there would be cuts in discretionary and travel spending. The idea, the sources who leaked the information said, would be to demonstrate that those in Ottawa were leading by example in these tough financial times. The right for civil servants to strike would be eliminated, and the government would sell off some of its assets to raise money.

When the financial update came, however, it contained a bombshell that set off a constitutional crisis in Canada that had never been seen before. Yes, the update did not include any kind of economic stimulus spending, as had been anticipated in the face of the worsening financial crisis. Yes, the update even went so far as to state that Canada would actually see a surplus—albeit a small one of $100 million—at the end of the fiscal year. But Flaherty and the Conservatives, in their biggest announcement, took direct aim at their political opponents and announced that they were taking away their money.

Specifically, Flaherty announced that the government would eliminate the public subsidy that each political party received. This subsidy was the lifeblood of almost all the political parties, except for the Conservatives. Each party was paid a specific amount based on their performance in the previous election. The math worked out to each party receiving approximately $1.95 per vote, which meant that millions of dollars were at stake.

"There will be no free ride for political parties. There never was. The freight was paid by the taxpayer. This is the last stop on the route," Flaherty said, making it known that the subsidy would cease to exist in April 2009.

It was bad news for every party but the Conservatives. Although they stood to lose the most—$9.1 million—based on their performance in the 2008 election, the party had raised $18 million nationally, meaning that the subsidy represented only about one-third of their total funding.

The Liberals, however, were in bad shape. Based on their performance in the last election, they stood to receive $6.4 million from the subsidy program. That represented almost two-thirds of their revenue, considering they had managed to garner only $4.7 million through fundraising. The party was also in debt to the tune of $1.6 million.

The subsidy amounts for the rest of Canada's political parties were less, but given the other parties' smaller budgets, the loss of the subsidy would be even more severe. The NDP was slated to receive $4.4 million, the Bloc Québécois $2.6 million and the Greens, who had yet to elect even a single candidate nationally, would lose $1.8 million.

The opposition was outraged and made it known immediately.

"This is huge. This is so audacious and outrageous. This is war," said Pat Martin (Winnipeg-Centre) of the NDP.

While the opposition parties made it clear that although they were unimpressed with both the lack of stimulus in the update and the idea that Canada could still finish the fiscal year in a surplus position, it was the loss of the subsidy that truly upset them. Specifically, the parties believed, and many media pundits later agreed, that Stephen Harper had picked an economically sensitive time to launch a partisan attack against his political enemies. Eliminating the per-vote subsidy could enshrine the Conservatives in power for years as they took advantage of their greater fundraising ability. What was particularly strange about the Conservative proposal was that they had not mentioned the idea of eliminating the subsidy once during the preceding election or during the Speech from the Throne.

"Every modern democracy has an element of public support for political parties," said Liberal MP Bob Rae. "The idea this would now be destroyed by the action of one government attempting to take advantage of an economic crisis to somehow turn it to their own partisan advantage is disgraceful, and for that alone this government just needs a wake-up call."

Yet no one could have predicted what would transpire next. All four of the major political parties had just finished a bruising six-week federal election the previous month, which had also been the third election in four years. They had shuttered their war rooms and returned the buses and planes. Their war chests were, if not exhausted, then pretty close to it. It was difficult to believe that any party, especially the parties of the opposition, would be interested in actually fighting another election.

Yet that's exactly what started to take shape. This was a minority government, and the opposition parties, who outnumbered the Conservatives, could defeat them at any time with a vote of non-confidence. Keeping the subsidy was so important to the opposition parties that they were willing to fight another election to try to keep it.

The opposition parties had another option available to them. If they defeated the Harper Conservatives with a vote of non-confidence, Harper would go the Governor General to tell her that he had lost the confidence of Parliament and request a new election. It was possible, though, that because the last election had taken place only the previous month, the Governor General would not send Canadians back to the polls. She could, instead, use her reserve powers to task one of the other parties in the House of Commons to attempt to form a government.

But there was a problem, and that problem specifically was Stéphane Dion. The Liberal leader was a lame duck, having already announced his desire to resign from his post the following spring. If the opposition parties were to offer themselves as an alternative to the current government, would Dion still resign or would he withdraw his resignation to serve as prime minister? Liberals behind the scenes, according to a few sources, actually went so far as to approach former prime minister Jean Chrétien to see if he could broker a meeting between Dion and leadership hopefuls Bob Rae and Michael Ignatieff to come up with a strategy in which Dion would not lead the Liberals into the next election.

There were never any illusions about what the opposition parties were fighting for—the end of the political subsidy could dramatically reshape how politics was carried out in Canada. Opposition MPs publicly criticized the lack of any kind of stimulus spending in the economic update, but no one believed for a second that that was the main reason for the opposition's displeasure.

"The onus now is really on Prime Minister Harper to consider his options, to consider his situation," said Liberal House leader Ralph Goodale. "He's put a so-called plan before Canadians this afternoon. It's not a plan to bolster the economy. It is a plan to hide a deficit. It's not acceptable, and he should reconsider his position."

The Liberals and the NDP immediately started conferring with one another at the advisor level, each wanting to see if the other was open to the idea of forming a coalition. Jack Layton cancelled travel plans and decided to stick around Ottawa in case he was needed. The first chance the opposition would have to vote down the government would be December 1, only a few days away, so the two sides needed to confer quickly.

A consensus started to emerge among the experts that the media interviewed about the growing crisis—it held that, considering it had been barely six weeks since the last election and Parliament had been sitting, at that point, for only eight days, Harper would be hard-pressed to convince the Governor General that an election, if he lost a confidence vote, was in the country's best interests. Presented with that kind of scenario, it was believed that Jean would almost certainly ask the opposition to try to form a government.

Only once in Canadian history had a Governor General been in the position of asking the opposition to do this. In 1925, Lord Byng, the Governor General of Canada, refused a request by then-Prime Minister William Lyon Mackenzie King to dissolve Parliament shortly after an election had already been held. Byng instead asked the Conservatives to form a government. The Conservatives promptly lost a confidence vote, and an election was called.

Dion had already tabled a motion of confidence in the House that read:

> *In light of the Conservatives' failure to recognize the seriousness of Canada's economic situation...this House has lost confidence in this government and is of the opinion that a viable alternative government can be formed within the present House of Commons.*

Harper decided to give himself and his Conservatives some breathing room. He used his powers to move the Liberals' opposition day, the day on which they could have had the House vote on their motion of non-confidence, from December 1 to December 8. He lashed out at the opposition parties for what they were doing.

"While we have been working on the economy, the opposition has been working on a backroom deal to overturn the results of the last election without seeking the consent of voters. They want to take power, not earn it," Harper said.

He made it clear that he did not believe the opposition should simply be allowed to form a government.

"The opposition has every right to defeat the government, but Stéphane Dion does not have the right to take power without an election. Canada's government should be decided by Canadians, not backroom deals," Harper said.

Despite his strong words, Harper tried to signal his intent to back off from the position his government had taken in the fiscal update. It was announced over the November 29–30 weekend that the Conservatives would bring a "comprehensive" budget to the House of Commons on January 27 and that the budget might contain "temporary stimulus" for the auto sector. The Conservatives also said they would forego their temporary ban on strikes in the public service and would get rid of their plan to eliminate the per-vote subsidy. Then, in an attempt to undermine the would-be coalition, the Conservatives released a transcript of a recent conference featuring Jack Layton of the NDP talking about how his party had some sort of arrangement in place with the Bloc Québécois to form a coalition to bring down the government.

But the opposition said that it was too late and, at the conclusion of the weekend, all three opposition parties signed an agreement that they would create an alternative coalition that could govern Canada once the Conservatives had been defeated. Under the agreement, which was predominately between the Liberals and NDP, Stéphane Dion would become prime minister until his successor was chosen in May. The Liberals would get 18 of 24 cabinet posts, including the coveted finance minister's post, while the NDP would get six cabinet posts and six parliamentary secretary positions to fill. The two parties would still caucus separately, but both would be able to meet jointly and offer advice to the government. They would consult with one another on appointments, and a standing committee of the accord forming the coalition would be created and chaired by the prime minister. The accord would expire in June 2011.

There would be two years of economic stimulus when the coalition took over, it was revealed. The stimulus money would be focused on infrastructure, housing construction and manufacturing. The stimulus spending would likely result in a deficit position, but the coalition would put policies in place to return Canada to a surplus in four years. The coalition also revealed that it would be advised in economic matters by a quartet of senior politicians—former Liberal premier of New Brunswick Frank McKenna, former NDP premier of Saskatchewan Roy Romanow, former Liberal finance minister John Manley and former Liberal finance minister and prime minister Paul Martin.

The Bloc Québécois had agreed to support the coalition for a period of 18 months. The accord between the Liberals and NDP also promised to create a "permanent way of consulting with the Bloc Québécois" during that time.

"Given the critical situation facing our fellow citizens and the refusal and inability of the Harper government to deal with this critical situation, the opposition parties have decided it was now time to take action," Dion said.

Once the accord was signed and public, Dion even took the step of writing a letter to the Governor General, who was travelling overseas on state business but was scheduled to return by the end of that week, advising her that the House had lost confidence in the Conservatives and that the opposition parties, as a coalition, were ready to step in if she would allow them to.

"This new government should be allowed to demonstrate it has the confidence of the House of Commons," the letter explained.

A meeting between the three Liberals who had already announced their intention to run for the party leadership in May—Dominic LeBlanc, Michael Ignatieff and Bob Rae—confirmed that Dion would serve as prime minister in the event the coalition was asked to form a government. The confirmation led to the press dubbing Dion "the accidental prime minister."

The impact of the crisis on the already toxic decorum in the House of Commons was significant, driving the MPs' behaviour toward one another to new lows. While members of the opposition were always quick to jeer any response in Question Period by the prime minister or one of his ministers, they now started jeering, applauding and mocking even the slightest error. At one point, while responding to a question, Harper briefly stumbled over his words as he was speaking. The mocking response of the opposition parties was deafening.

But the Conservatives behaved no better—with the coalition now assured the support of the Bloc Québécois, the Conservatives started pounding away at the Bloc's support of the coalition, framing the alliance as a deal between the opposition parties and the separatists.

"This is a coalition that's supported by separatists, people who would break up our country," said Environment Minister Jim Prentice. "This is a serious situation. It is irresponsible and undemocratic."

Harper used similar responses in Question Period.

"The deal that the leader of the Liberal Party has made with the separatists is a betrayal of the voters of this country, a betrayal of the best interests of our economy, a betrayal of the best interests of our country, and we will fight it with every means we have," Harper thundered in one Question Period response. But he went even further while giving remarks at a Conservative Christmas party, saying that what the opposition parties were doing was illegal, even though it wasn't.

"We will use all legal means to resist this undemocratic seizure of power," he told Conservative staffers.

The entire affair was starting to put Harper in a negative light, and speculation was mounting that if the government fell, Harper would have to resign as Conservative leader. Even media pundits typically sympathetic to the Conservatives were baffled by what Harper had done—using an economically sensitive time for all Canadians to try to hit his opponents in the wallet, all under the auspices of trying to help the country in the midst of a global financial crisis. It was disingenuous, they said, given that Harper had never before raised the possibility of doing anything about the voting subsidy. The Conservatives decided to start getting ready for a possible election, reopening their war room and putting deposits down on buses and airplanes for an election campaign.

However, the Conservatives had also come up with a strategy for avoiding a confidence vote in the House—proroguing Parliament. To prorogue Parliament meant to end the current session. Parliament was typically prorogued when a government had achieved all of its legislative goals. The House would no longer sit, all committee work would cease and all unapproved legislation would die on the order paper. All the politicians would be sent home and would not have to campaign in an election. After the prorogue was over, there would be a Speech from the Throne, which would signal the opening of a new session of Parliament.

The wild card in seeking a prorogation was the Governor General, who was on her way back to Canada. It had been only two weeks since the Speech from the Throne had opened the current session. Harper could not possibly claim that the Conservatives had achieved all of their legislative goals for that session. And it was not known how the Governor General would react to the fact that Harper was, basically, proroguing Parliament to avoid a confidence vote.

If Jean did not permit Harper to prorogue the House, it would mean facing a confidence vote the Conservatives were certain to lose. And if that happened, Jean had two options—she could dissolve Parliament and send Canadians back to the polls, or she could exercise her reserve power to ask the opposition to form a government.

On the night of December 3, with Harper scheduled to meet with the Governor General the following morning at 9:30, the leaders of both the Conservatives and the Liberals decided to take their case directly to Canadians in a pair of broadcasts. In an approximately five-minute, pre-recorded address, Stephen Harper talked about the economic crisis and how the government was going to do something about it when the Conservatives brought their budget forward in January. He tried to warn Canadians about the dangers of the coalition and its association with the Bloc Québécois.

"Instead of an immediate budget, they propose a new coalition which includes the party in Parliament whose avowed goal is to break up the country. Let me be very clear: Canada's government cannot enter into a power-sharing coalition with a separatist party," Harper said.

This statement, of course, made no reference to the Conservative's past instances of colluding with the Bloc Québécois to try to bring down the Liberal government in previous years. But Harper continued on.

"The opposition is attempting to impose this deal without your say, without your consent and without your vote. This is no time for backroom deals with separatists; it is time for Canada's government to focus on the economy and specifically on measures for the upcoming budget."

He then appealed to Canadians' sense of patriotism.

"This is a pivotal moment in our history. We Canadians are the inheritors of a great legacy, and it is our duty to strengthen and protect it for the generations still to come. Tonight I pledge to you that Canada's government will use every legal means at our disposal to protect our democracy, to protect our economy and to protect Canada.

Harper then signed off and Canadians waited. Stéphane Dion's address to Canada was supposed to come immediately after Harper's, but several minutes passed, and nothing happened. News anchors on the networks started to kill time. It turned out that the Liberals' address had not yet arrived. By the time it came, CTV had already decided to return to its regularly scheduled programming.

But that wasn't the end of the fiasco with the Liberals' address. When it arrived, there was only an English version—no French version had been taped, so Liberal staffers were forced to edit a French tape on the spot (Stephen Harper had done his address in both French and English). When the video finally hit the airwaves, it was of incredibly poor quality.

"The Harper Conservatives have lost the confidence of the majority of members of the House of Commons. In our democracy, in our parliamentary system, in our constitution, this means they have lost the right to govern," Dion said in the address.

The next morning, Stephen Harper met with Governor General Michaëlle Jean to discuss proroguing the House. At its conclusion, Jean granted Harper his prorogue, but under two conditions—that he brought Parliament back sooner rather than later, and that he bring forward a budget that that would win support in the House of Commons. Harper agreed to both conditions.

Years later, one of Jean's advisors, constitutional scholar Peter Russell, said Jean was afraid that refusing Harper's request would lead to a deeper crisis of government for Canadians.

"I think her reasons were that parliamentary democracy is going to be protected sufficiently to avoid a dangerous and dreadful crisis by giving an affirmative answer to the prime minister," Russell said.

Parliament would return on January 26, Harper said, with the budget still scheduled to come down on January 27.

"The public is very frustrated with the situation in Parliament. We are all responsible," Harper said. He claimed that the break would allow his party to focus on protecting the economy.

"The opposition criticism is that we have to focus on the economy immediately. Today's decision will give us an opportunity…to focus on the economy and to work together," Harper said.

The coalition leaders were, naturally, unimpressed and remained stoic in their commitment to defeating the government.

"[Harper] put a lock on the door of the House of Commons, and he refused to face the people of Canada through their elected representatives," Layton said.

But as bruised and battered as Harper looked at the end of the crisis, Dion fared far worse. He had come under significant criticism for his handling of the crisis, especially within his own party. The Liberals were not happy that Dion, a staunch federalist, had made a deal with the Bloc Québécois. They were not happy that Dion had not allowed any criticism of the coalition within the party ranks. And they were especially upset over the amateurish video that had ended up running late on the networks the night before. Speculation began to mount that most Liberals did not want to go to the polls anytime soon with him as leader. And with another confidence vote coming in January when the Conservatives brought forward their budget, there was a possibility that would happen.

On December 8, the Liberals announced that Dion would step down immediately so that his successor, whoever that would be, could lead the party into January and the unveiling of the Conservative budget. That way, the party would be prepared for an election should one occur.

"We need to have a new leader in place by then. We need to have the leadership race moved up," Rae said.

But it wasn't going to be Rae who was the leader. Shortly after it was announced that Dion was stepping down immediately, Rae announced that he was withdrawing from the leadership race. Dominic Leblanc had already withdrawn. That left Michael Ignatieff as the new Liberal leader.

However, with Ignatieff in the driver's seat, the coalition was at risk. Ignatieff was a not a fan of taking down the Conservatives at any cost. He went so far as to say that if the budget brought forward by the Conservatives in January was in the national interest, he would ask the Liberals to support it. But he was also not afraid to vote it down.

"He must not doubt my calm, quiet determination that he has to walk back down the hill," Ignatieff said of Harper.

Everyone headed home for Christmas. Well, almost everyone. Harper stayed behind long enough to fill 18 Senate seats with patronage appointments, despite his expressed desire in previous years to reform how the Red Chamber was run. Among the 18 Conservative friends named to plum positions were three who would later become thorns in Harper's side: former TV journalists Pamela Wallin and Mike Duffy, and Patrick Brazeau, leader of the Congress of Aboriginal Peoples.

On January 27, the Conservatives unveiled their budget. It contained a two-year, $40-billion economic recovery plan that involved infrastructure spending, tax cuts and home-renovation incentives. Conservatives boasted that it would actually boost growth by 1.2 percent and avert a recession. The budget included $1.5 billion for skills training and $125 billion to improve the availability of credit, and would create 190,000 jobs over two years. Furthermore, unlike the rosy fiscal update that had promised the government would stay in a surplus position, it forecasted deficits totalling $84.9 billion over the next five years.

The Bloc and the NDP quickly rejected the budget, but Ignatieff asked for, and received, an assurance from the Harper government that it would provide three accountability reports on the effectiveness of the stimulus strategies. The Conservatives agreed.

"We are putting the government on probation," Ignatieff said when he announced his party's support for the budget. "We will be watching them like hawks to make sure the investments Canadians need actually reach them."

With that support, the coalition was officially dead. The crisis that had seemed so real and possible a mere six weeks earlier was over. But the seeds of another crisis had been sown in the Senate appointments that had taken place.

CHAPTER SIX

F-35 Purchase Scandal

Whether they were seated in the opposition benches or trying to convince Canadian voters to give them a shot at government, the Conservatives usually trumpeted the same basic virtues—transparency in government, accountability in office and being fiscally responsible with taxpayer dollars. The debacle that became the F-35 acquisition scandal was a dagger in the heart of all three.

There is no question that Canada needs to replace its stock of fighter jets sooner rather than later. After all, the current stock of CF-18 Hornets have been patrolling the Canadian skies and serving the Royal Canadian Air Force since 1982, when McDonnell Douglas started deliveries of the CF-18. The purchase of CF-18s actually began in 1977, when the government held its New Fighter Aircraft competition. Candidates in that particular competition included the Grumman F-14 Tomcat, the McDonnell Douglas F-15 Eagle, the Panavia Tornado, the Dassault Mirage 2000, the General Dynamics F-16, a lighter version of the F/A-18 called the F-18L and the F/A-18. That list was eventually whittled down to a shortlist of three—the F-16, the F-18L and the F/A-18. The government ended up selecting the F/A-18, which was dubbed the CF-18, and placed an order for 98 single-seat CF-18s and 40 dual-seat CF-18s for a total cost of $4 billion.

One important item to note from the selection of the CF-18 is that it was chosen as part of an open competition. In this competition, the RCAF created a list of criteria that were distributed to the different companies taking part in the competition. Those companies then responded with pitches for their particular aircraft, including a purchase price. In competitions, the company with the lowest price that meets the listed criteria is typically selected. Consequently, holding a competition ensures that the purchaser, whoever it might be, is getting a fair price for the product. Competition, in other words, drives prices down. And when it comes to military contracts, which can reach into the billions of dollars, getting the lowest possible price is critical, especially when you are spending taxpayer dollars.

The purchase of goods from an outside source is called procurement. And military procurement can get very complicated very quickly. As an illustration, one need look no further than the previous Liberal government and the ongoing saga of Canada's naval helicopters. The navy has been operating the Sikorsky CH-124 Sea King helicopter from its ships since 1963. The need for a replacement was identified as early as 1985, which led to a competition among three contenders—the Sikorsky S-70 SeaHawk, the Aérospatiale AS332F Super Puma and the AugustaWestland EH-101. Sikorsky eventually withdrew from the competition, and in 1987, at the end of the competition, the government announced it would buy 35 of the EH-101s. It added 15 to that total to replace its CH-113 search and rescue helicopters. The estimated total cost was $5.8 billion. That number was later reduced in the face of budgetary pressures to buy 43 helicopters in total for $4.4 billion.

But in the ensuing election in 1993, Liberal leader Jean Chrétien famously announced that, if elected, he would cancel the contract, which he did when the Liberals won. The government was forced to pay AugustaWestland $500 million in cancellation fees. As a result, there was no move made to replace the Sea Kings until Chrétien retired 10 years later. Sikorsky's H-92 SeaHawk won the subsequent competition, and the aircraft was dubbed the CH-148 Cyclone.

But to this day, no helicopters have been deployed, costing Sikorsky almost $90 million in late fees, and its date of delivery was pushed from 2008 to 2015. The total cost for the replacement has almost doubled since the deal was approved, from $3.1 billion to $5.7 billion. Former Auditor General Sheila Fraser, in one of her last reports, slammed the Department of National Defence (DND) for lowballing costs on the Cyclone purchase and for claiming that the helicopter was going to be an "off-the-shelf" model when it knew very well that modifications would be required—modifications to the helicopter for Canada's purposes increased the cost of each aircraft by 70 percent over the initial quote.

Yet when the Conservative government announced quite suddenly in July 2010 that it would buy the F-35 Lightning II as the replacement for the CF-18, there was no mention of any kind of competition. Delivery of the F-35 to the RCAF would start in 2016. The decision to spend approximately $9 billion to purchase 65 of the new stealth fighter jets seemed to come completely out of the blue. The total cost announced that day was actually $16 billion, tacking on another $7 billion to the original purchase price for 20 years' worth of maintenance. But Defence Minister Peter MacKay insisted that the F-35 was the plane that Canada needed for the RCAF.

"We need an aircraft that can enable the men and women of the Canadian Forces to meet the increasingly complex demands of the missions that we ask of them," MacKay said at an Ottawa news conference, flanked by Public Works Minister Rona Ambrose and Industry Minister Tony Clement.

The selection of the F-35 as Canada's fighter of the future was a surprise, but not a big one. The F-35 had emerged out of a program called the Joint Strike Fighter (JSF) program in the United States, which had the goal of trying to find a plane to replace several different aircraft in use in the United States Armed Forces. The goal was to design a cutting-edge, common airframe that could be used by the U.S. Air Force, Navy and Marines. Two manufacturers submitted prototype aircraft for the competition—Boeing submitted its X-32 aircraft, and Lockheed Martin entered its X-35. The U.S. military selected the X-35 as the aircraft of the future in 2001, at which time development began. There would be three different versions of the aircraft—the F-35A would be a standard airframe, the F-35B would have short take-off and vertical landing (STOVL) abilities like the Harrier jet operated by the Marines, and the F-35C would be built for operating on and off aircraft carriers. All variants would be "stealth" fighters, capable of evading enemy radar and conducting air-to-air or air-to-ground warfare, as well as carrying all their weapons internally with mounts on the wings for additional weapons.

Canada was a participant in the JSF program early on. Participation in the program at that time did not marry Canada to purchasing the F-35 in the future, but it did keep it involved in the development of the aircraft and also allowed Canadian companies to bid on contracts related to the F-35. The Canadian government had already signed two memorandums of understanding (MOU)—one in 2002, committing $100 million to the development of the F-35, and a second in 2006, committing the government to spending up to $551 million on the aircraft's development.

So from that perspective, MacKay's announcement wasn't much of a surprise. The surprise came in how the government came to decide on the F-35 as its future fighter aircraft. When it selected the CF-18, the military had held a competition among various manufacturers to ensure that it received the right airplane at the best possible price. In the case of the F-35, there hadn't been a competition. When pressed on this point, MacKay stated that the selection had been made after a "rigorous process" that he claimed had actually started when the previous Liberal government had been in power. That wasn't entirely true, even though the Conservatives trotted the point out to counter Liberal criticism of the decision—the Liberals, who had signed the original MOU for $100 million, had been involved in research and development. They had never made a formal commitment to purchase the aircraft.

"There is absolutely no rush to move this…in the dead of summer with zero accountability," Liberal defence critic Ujjal Dosanjh argued.

With maintenance factored in, the total $16 billion cost worked out to roughly $140 million per aircraft, or $75 million for the aircraft alone. The cost was, at first glance, higher than what it would cost the United States, but MacKay said that was because the Canadian planes, which would be called CF-35s, would include sensors and weapons systems.

The potential industry benefits for Canadian companies were attractive. The F-35 program was effectively an eight-country partnership that would likely result in the construction of an estimated 3000 aircraft. Roughly 85 Canadian companies, research laboratories and universities had already netted $350 million in contracts, and there might be billions more at stake.

The F-35 program, however, had been openly criticized in the United States since the start of the plane's development following the competition. The plane was seen as being too expensive, too slow and not stealthy enough, and it would have a tough time defending itself against advanced fighters from enemy countries such as Russia.

There were domestic critics of the plane as well. First, some criticized spending $16 billion on fighters when the Conservatives had put the country into a $50 million deficit. Others were skeptical that the F-35 was, in fact, the right plane for Canada. The first, most obvious and, to some, most critical problem with the F-35 was the fact that it was a single-engine aircraft. The CF-18 was a twin-engine plane. Having two engines, especially when operating in a large country with such inhospitable conditions as those encountered in the North, was seen as insurance against possible engine problems. If one engine quit or had to be shut down in flight, the pilot could still nurse his CF-18 home on the remaining engine. With a single-engine plane, if the engine quit, the pilot would have no choice but to eject. And in the middle of the Arctic, that pilot might be faced with severe challenges in staying alive until help came. The twin-engine was the reason the CF-18 had been chosen over the F-16 Fighting Falcon when the previous competition for fighter aircraft had been held in Canada—the F-16 was also a single-engine aircraft.

No sooner had Canada made the announcement of its intention to purchase the F-35 than aerospace companies the world over started to clamour for an open competition. The likes of Boeing, with its F/A-18 Super Hornet, an upgrade over the CF-18, and Eurofighter, with its Typhoon fighter, made it known that they wanted to pit their plane against the F-35.

In retaliation, the DND and the Conservatives pointed out that the F-35 was what was called a "fifth-generation fighter," whereas the rest were merely "fourth-generation fighters." The key distinction between a fourth-generation and a fifth-generation fighter was stealth. Boeing's F/A-18 Super Hornet, Eurofighter's Typhoon, Saab's Griffen and Dassault's Rafale were good airplanes, but none had the stealth characteristics of the F-35; a factoid trumpeted by F-35 proponents was that it had the radar cross-section of a golf ball, meaning that it was unlikely to appear on enemy radar. It was also the only fifth-generation fighter available for sale within NATO. There was one other fifth-generation airplane—the F-22 Raptor—operated by the United States, but it was not available for export. That left the F-35 as the only fifth-generation fighter available for Canada to actually buy. The government also held that because the United States was buying so many of the planes and so many NATO allies were planning to buy the F-35, it meant that the countries operating the plane would be better able to support one another in combat missions.

Those facts didn't appease the opposition, however. Within days of the announcement, Dosanjh called for a probe into the decision by the Conservatives to pursue a "sole-source" procurement of the F-35, meaning that no competition had been held. He directed his call for a probe to Kevin Page, the Parliamentary Budget Officer (PBO), who was already a pain the side of the Conservatives.

Within weeks of the announcement, there was a strange development online with respect to Canada's decision to buy the F-35. It emerged that around July 20, an unknown person or people had tried to make changes to the Wikipedia page about the JSF program. Wikipedia is, of course, an online encyclopedia edited by computer users. Specifically, it was discovered that those nine attempts all related to removing or changing any information about the F-35 purchase by Canada that was critical of the Conservative government. There were also attempts made to insert insults aimed at Liberal leader Michael Ignatieff, who, along with his party, openly questioned the purchase. Quotes from Michael Byers, a professor at the University of British Columbia, who had opposed the purchase, were also removed.

Wikipedia responded by locking down the page, meaning that only editors recognized by Wikipedia could edit the page from that point on. Wikipedia also decided to trace who had tried to change the page. They were able to establish that the attempts to make the changes had occurred during normal work hours. They were also able to trace the computers involved in the attempts to the DND, specifically to the offices of Defence, Research and Development Canada.

"It sounds to me like someone was freelancing. This is not behaviour we commonly condone," said DND spokesperson Martin Champoux. He said there was no concerted attempt by the DND as a whole to remove criticism of the purchase. He also said that department IT specialists were looking for the people who might have used the computers at those times.

The government was not actually bound to the purchase of the F-35s, the Conservatives were quick to point out as criticism of the purchase started to mount. It had not signed a contract yet, but had instead signed another MOU. But as experts continued to comb through the contract, the more bothered they became. The lack of competition, some critics pointed out, meant that Canada was likely going to end up paying more for the F-35 than if they had chosen it through a competition. Even if they selected the F-35 at the end of the competition, they would likely have gotten a cheaper price on it than they did by pursuing it through a sole-source contract.

"The sole-sourcing was stupid," one DND source said to the *National Post*. "It was in the country's interests to hold an open competition and invite four manufacturers to hawk their wares. We didn't go through this process. Peter MacKay says there was a competition, but there was only an internal study. That means we'll never be able to determine how much they would have reduced their price or the scope of industrial benefits they would have offered."

Those industrial benefits were also open to questioning—there was no guarantee that by buying the F-35, Canadian businesses would actually get any of the contracts that would be up for grabs. Yet the

Conservatives still kept plugging the possibility of contracts for Canadian businesses as a major part of the reason for purchasing the F-35.

"We're getting access to compete on contracts for up to 5000 airplanes that aren't being purchased in Canada; they're being pursued by other member nations," Rona Ambrose said, adding that any government that pulled out of the deal was risking at least $12 billion in potential contract opportunities.

In September 2010, when the House of Commons resumed sitting after the summer break and after the announcement had been made, the House Committee on National Defence held hearings into the purchase of the F-35. The hearings were called for by opposition MPs on the committee who questioned the need for the purchase. Peter MacKay was one of the first witnesses. He stressed the need for Canada to replace their CF-18s before they reached the end of their lifespan.

"An operational gap, I stress, is not an option," MacKay said. He also called the F-35 the "most affordable option" of the jets available on the market.

When the lack of a competition was put to Rona Ambrose as being fundamentally wrong, she replied that there was no sense in holding a competition because the F-35 was the only real alternative.

"It would be dishonest. It would be a waste of time, and it would be a waste of resources," Ambrose said.

Following Ambrose, Minister of Industry Tony Clement told the committee that not purchasing the plane would mean that Canadian companies would not receive privileged access to the JSF program.

But a raft of documents obtained by the *Ottawa Citizen* showed that the military brass and those involved in the procurement for a new fighter had been expecting a competition in 2010. While MacKay had emphasized the need to act immediately to buy the jets to make sure they were in the RCAF's hands before the CF-18s reached the end of their lifespan, the documents showed very little concern for any kind of "operational gap." A competition in 2010 would have yielded a contract to the winning company in 2012. Delivery would have begun in 2015–16, with the planes fully operational between 2018 and 2023. That timeline was very similar to what the government was proposing with its sole-source procurement of the F-35.

The Conservatives also tried to make the point that a competition had been held between Boeing and Lockheed Martin for the right to make the JSF, and that Lockheed Martin had won that competition. They also called attention to the fact that Canada had been a partner of the program in 2001, when the competition took place. Critics, however, were quick to point out that the competition had been to meet the needs of the United States military. It had not been a competition to meet Canada's military needs.

The early news about the F-35 from the testing grounds was also not good. The project was already behind schedule and over budget in the United States, and it was running into problems. In October 2010, it was revealed that a software glitch in the fuel pump had grounded the entire test fleet for a period of time before flights were eventually restarted. Accounting problems with Lockheed Martin had caused the company to lose its Pentagon certification until that problem was fixed. Some of Canada's allies started to get cold feet—Norway had already pushed back its plan to buy the F-35 by two years. The per-plane price was jumping wildly around with no predictable estimate available. Some estimates came in at $50 million and others at $92 million per plane, with some as high as $135 million. The Conservatives said that they were actually hoping to get a small break on the per-plane price because Canada's aircraft would be manufactured between 2016 and 2022, when Lockheed Martin would be at peak production for the F-35.

Critics of the F-35 program eventually found a champion with the background and credentials to be taken seriously. Alan Williams was a retired Deputy Minister of Materials who had worked for the public service for 33 years and had been part of the 2002 MOU in which Canada had committed $100 million. He had even written a book on procurement entitled, *Reinventing Canadian Defence Procurement: A View from the Inside*. He was highly critical of the purchase.

Williams testified at a defence committee hearing, "Procurement demands not only the highest degree of integrity, but also the appearance of the highest degree of integrity. Undertaking sole-source deals leaves the procurement process more vulnerable to fraud, bribery and behind-the-scene deal-making and leaves the federal government more susceptible to such charges."

Prime Minister Stephen Harper responded to the criticism as he typically does to negative statements of any kind—he started to undermine Williams' reputation and attack his character.

"In terms of the individual you are talking about, his advice was very different at the time he was actually paid to give it," Harper replied during a media scrum when asked about Williams' remarks.

"That's a lie. I've never changed my opinion about sole-sourcing. I have no idea what he's referring to. I take great offence to that," Williams said in response to Harper's remarks.

The country got a good look at the kind of messes that procurement can create in late October 2010, when Auditor General Sheila Fraser released one of her scathing reports on government spending. She had not yet had time to examine the F-35, but she had just finished looking at the books on the CH-148 Cyclone purchase. The entire process, as discussed at the beginning of this chapter, had been a debacle from start to finish and led to the per-helicopter price increasing by as much as 70 percent because costs had been low-balled. Fraser pointed out that the department responsible for the Cyclone purchase was the same department that would be responsible for the F-35 purchase. She warned that the fighter procurement faced the same risks that had plagued the Cyclone procurement.

"Let's hope no one's assessing [the F-35s] as low risk," Fraser said during a press conference on her report.

Days later, the Liberals made the totality of their opposition to the program known when Michael Ignatieff announced that a Liberal government would cancel the project outright and hold a competitive bid because of the problems with the Cyclone purchase that Sheila Fraser had noted in her report.

"We are convinced that a fully competitive bid, with a clear definition of what the strategic and military needs of this aircraft are, will get us a lot better value for money," Ignatieff said.

There was more news that opened the F-35 purchase to further criticism. First came reports that the F-35s would likely require modifications to improve its range for Canada's purposes or Canada would have to look at spending hundreds of millions either on new refuelling aircraft or on modifications to its existing refuelling aircraft because the F-35 was not compatible with them. Then came unfortunate news out of the United Kingdom—the country was looking at cutting its order of F-35s from 138 to 50.

The United States, despite the problems with the F-35, was still trying to keep its allies on board with the program. In a visit to Canada to meet with Peter MacKay, U.S. Secretary of Defense Robert Gates said that Canada's participation in the program was important.

"Obviously, having all our partners continue to be with us in this program is very important and I'm pleased at the number of our allies who are going with the F-35. It is a true fifth-generation fighter, it will give us significant capabilities, it will continue the interoperability that has been at the heart of our NORAD relationship for decades now."

The Conservatives continued to mount attacks against their critics, most notably Alan Williams. Conservative MP Laurie Hawn, himself a former RCAF fighter pilot, began circulating emails to supporters and journalists in which he described Williams' criticism of the procurement for the F-35 as "BS."

"He doesn't want to debate the issues. Instead, he just attacks the individual," Williams retaliated.

The sharpest criticism came on March 10, 2011, when Kevin Page, the Parliamentary Budget Officer, released his report on the F-35 procurement. The numbers were eye-popping. His first point of contention was with the lifespan of the F-35—the government had given a 20-year timeframe and a $7 billion price tag associated with maintenance costs. Page's numbers were different. He figured that the total cost of buying and operating 65 F-35s was closer to $29.3 billion over 30 years, almost double the cost for 10 additional years. The report did not look at the quality of the aircraft, only at its costs. Page's report estimated a purchase price of $9.7 billion for the 65 planes, almost $700 million more than the government's estimates. It also looked at the expense of retrofitting air bases to handle the F-35, which the DND had not done, and examined the costs of overhauls and upgrades. Page took aim at the assertion that Canadian businesses could profit from the purchase of the jets, saying that buying the F-35 did not guarantee domestic contracts for purchasing countries. He criticized the sole-source procurement method, saying that sole-sourced purchases could cost approximately 20 percent more than products purchased through a competition.

The DND responded with what the public already suspected—in preparing its initial estimate, it had not undertaken a thorough analysis of costs for the F-35.

Page's report led to increased demands for the Conservatives to share more information about the potential costs of the F-35 purchase, but the government was not forthcoming. In the prior month, some members of the opposition had asked Speaker Peter Milliken to rule on the issue of the government not turning over documents that had been requested.

Milliken had already ruled on the supremacy of Parliament to request documents in the Afghan detainee scandal, but said he would rule again. The government turned over some documents shortly afterward, but they were deemed insufficient. On February 28, 2011, the opposition voted on and passed another motion ordering the government to hand over documents to the finance committee. They accused the government of withholding information because it would be politically embarrassing for them. The motion also gave the Conservatives a March 7 deadline for providing the documents, which they did not honour. On March 9, Milliken ruled that the documents provided to date were not enough to satisfy the House and that the government, for this and other reasons, could be found in contempt of Parliament.

He directed those matters to committee. On March 21, a report by the Procedure and House Affairs Committee stated that "the government's failure to produce documents constitutes a contempt of Parliament."

On March 25, the Conservatives were found by the House of Commons to be in contempt of Parliament and non-confidence in the government was declared, which led to an election—one the Conservatives would go on to win, giving them majority status in the House for the first time under Stephen Harper.

The F-35 became an issue during the election as the costs of the plane continued to pinball around. On March 31, the U.S. General Accountability Office (GAO) stated that the per-plane cost would be closer to $115 million instead of the $75 million figure that the Conservatives had used. That forced the DND to admit later in April that the $75 million price tag it had quoted to the Conservatives was no longer accurate.

Problems with the airplane itself were still mounting. Members of the U.S. Congress, frustrated with the ongoing delays and cost increases, openly mused about shutting the program down entirely. There were reports that the aircraft might have problems communicating in the Far North in Canada, a serious issue for a plane that would be spending a considerable amount of time patrolling that area of the country. Heading into November 2011, word of a new delay came, one of up to two years, that could increase the price of the plane. The F-35 was already five years behind schedule, but the Conservatives said that a delay in delivery from 2016 to 2018 wouldn't be problematic, except for the fact that Canada might not receive the last of its F-35s until 2022, two years after the CF-18s were scheduled to reach the end of their service lives. Weeks later, in December, the United States revealed problems with major cracks and flaws in the fighter's airframe.

Bad news for the F-35 continued to mount. In January 2012, Japan announced that it would buy only 42 of the fighters. A month later, the Pentagon cancelled the purchase of 14 fighters for the following year as a budget-saving measure and was looking at delaying the purchase of 179 more for a couple of years. The United Kingdom announced that it would buy fewer F-35s than originally planned but would not decide how many until 2015. Australia stated that it was reviewing its order and was buying 24 Boeing F/A-18 Super Hornets as a stopgap measure because of the delays with the F-35. Turkey halved the number of planes it had planned to purchase. Italy announced that it was rethinking its order, and the Netherlands had put its plan to buy 85 of the planes on hold.

It was a nonstop flow of bad news. Canada responded by floating the idea of using armed drones to either replace or augment the F-35s or to fill the gap if there were more delays. The DND was already preparing to order six Reaper drones at $30 million each. Liberal Senator Colin Kenney, a member of the Senate's Standing Committee on National Security and Defence, wrote in an op-ed piece that using drones wasn't practical.

"Down the line, drones will be able to do everything that pilot-flown jets do today. But that isn't going to happen anytime soon and certainly not before our fleet of CF-18 fighter jets have been retired. We would be well advised to buy fighter jets, even if (due to cost or technical concerns) they are not F-35s," Kenney wrote.

The government started to change its tune. In his testimony to the House defence committee on March 13, 2012, Julian Fantino, associate defence minister, told the committee that they hadn't ruled out simply walking away from the deal.

"The determinate decision has not yet been made as to whether or not we are going to actually purchase, buy or acquire the F-35. We have not yet discounted the possibility of backing out of the program," Fantino said.

Others involved in the procurement process weren't so quick to back away from the F-35.

"We continue to monitor the options available to us around the world," Dan Ross, head of military procurement for the DND, told the committee. "We really don't see any change in what's available out there."

On March 16, the finance committee finally received the documentation it had requested from the Conservative government. The documentation arrived a few weeks before the new Auditor General, Michael Ferguson, was scheduled to release his report into the F-35 procurement and confirmed that DND officials had glossed over warnings about scheduling and cost problems when they were trying to sell the government on the F-35 in 2010. A series of slides in the document put a great deal of emphasis on the F-35's benefits as opposed to those of its fourth-generation peers, as well as the possible industry benefits. The fact that the program was behind schedule was only briefly mentioned—only 54 of 298 test flights had been conducted in 2009, and the program as a whole was 11,000 hours behind schedule. The picture the documents painted was of DND officials choosing the aircraft they wanted, writing the requirements for it after the fact and leading the government around by the nose.

"The whole process was twisted to suit the needs of the military, with the acknowledgment and support of ministers. It really was totally unacceptable," Alan Williams said, when asked for his opinion.

Other documents made it pretty clear that the F-35 was not the only favourite. Reports showing the number of meetings that had been held with each aerospace manufacturer showed clear favouritism for Lockheed Martin, the manufacturer of the F-35. Lockheed Martin got the most meetings and face time, and it was the only company invited to meet with the chief of the air staff and with the parliamentary secretary for defence.

More negative reports came out about the F-35's problems. One revealed that the aircraft's skin, which was made of a special material called a fibre mat that was cured onto the surfaces of the plane, was subject to peeling and bubbling. The finding resulted in the entire test fleet being restricted to a top speed of Mach 1. It was also noted that the fibre mat was difficult to replace and repair.

As the date for the release of the Auditor General's report drew closer and the rumblings about the F-35 grew increasingly negative, the Conservatives took action. They put a freeze on spending on the F-35 and committed to providing annual updates to Parliament on the program's progress. The Conservatives made the rather radical decision of taking the file away from the DND's procurement officials and instead made Public Works the lead department on the file, even creating a new secretariat within Public Works to do so. At first called the F-35 Secretariat, it was later renamed the National Fighter Procurement Secretariat, to avoid the appearance that the outcome of the process had already been determined. The report also committed to a review of alternatives to the F-35, which would be performed by a four-person panel.

Auditor General Michael Ferguson released his report on April 3, 2012. If the findings in Kevin Page's report had been eye-popping, then those in Ferguson's were stupefying. Ferguson stated that the DND had failed to fully inform the minister and parliamentarians about the full costs and risks of the program. Ferguson's report stated:

> *Problems relating to the development of the F-35 were not fully communicated to decision-makers and risks*

> *presented to decision-makers did not reflect the problems the JSF program was experiencing at the time. Full life-cycle costs were understated in the estimates provided to support the government's decision to buy the F-35.*

His review of the briefing materials revealed that between 2006 and 2010, those in charge were not kept informed of the problems and risks in the program. In 2008, Ferguson found, the DND had concluded that the F-35 represented the "best value" aircraft but had no documentation to support that conclusion. He pointed out that the projection of the life cycle that the Conservatives had used for the plane—$16 billion over 20 years—fell well short of the estimated 36-year lifespan of each plane. He also noted that Canada might need to buy 14 additional planes to compensate for losses and attrition, something the Conservatives had not mentioned. His report accused the DND of hiding the real cost of the F-35 by not publicly stating the $10 billion in costs for operations. He claimed that the Conservatives likely knew in advance of the May 2011 election that the true cost was closer to $25 billion.

Ferguson also took aim at the idea that participating in the program would reap industrial benefits for Canadian companies:

> *These projections were not independently validated by federal departments, and in fact, this validation was difficult to do since the data is largely proprietary. We are concerned, because these projections were used to support key decisions related to Canada's participation in the JSF program and the purchase of the F-35.*

After reading the report, Thomas Mulcair, leader of the NDP, said that the F-35 program was "a litany of poor public administration, bad decision-making and a lack of accountability."

Williams was happy to read the Auditor General's findings.

"The military is responsible for developing the requirements. After that, they venture somewhere they're not competent. The civilians abdicated their responsibility—they have the responsibility to question and challenge, not to give the military what they want," Williams said.

Peter MacKay's response to the Auditor General likened the F-35 to buying a new car.

"If you went out and bought yourself a new minivan and you wanted to drive it off the lot, you wouldn't calculate the gas, the washer fluid, the oil and give yourself a salary to drive it for the next 15 to 20 years," MacKay said.

"I am concerned with suggestions that accurate estimation and the inclusion of personnel, operating and maintenance costs are not important, since they would be incurred regardless of the aircraft selected to replace the CF-18," Ferguson replied to MacKay's statement.

The Conservatives responded that the 2006 MOU had created such a commitment that they could not possibly hold a competition, a contention that Williams was quick to point out as being incorrect. The MOU simply laid out the rules that firms in partner countries had to follow to bid on work to build, assemble and equip the fighter.

Yet despite all the criticism of the program, no one in either the DND or the Conservative government made public the RCAF's statement of requirements for any new aircraft—no one knew exactly what the RCAF was looking for in its next fighter jet.

Two weeks later, in an op-ed piece, Liberal MP Marc Garneau took the Conservatives to task for their handling of the file.

"To this day, Canadians have not been shown a clearly stated set of requirements for the CF-18 replacement. Instead, they have been told that Canada needs the only "fifth-generation" aircraft available—a requirement which, as the Auditor General points out, is not an operational one," Garneau wrote.

He continued on to say that the Conservatives had failed completely on the F-35 file.

"The government has failed to tell us what mission capabilities it expects from the CF-18 replacement. It failed to hold an open competition in order to select the best aircraft possible based on performance, cost, availability and industrial benefits. Finally, it has failed to accept any responsibility whatsoever," Garneau wrote.

Critics of the F-35 continued to pile on.

"How do you get a single-engine, low-range, low-payload, low-manoeuvrability aircraft that is being optimized for close air support to operate effectively in the North?" asked Paul Maillet, a retired RCAF CF-18 fleet manager and former Green Party candidate.

The Public Accounts Committee (PAC) held hearings and learned more about the constantly changing cost of the aircraft. The DND had finally put away its $75 million price tag and was now saying the planes would cost $85 million each, even as the United States GAO put the cost at $137 million per plane.

Kevin Page was even asked to testify at the PAC, where he stated that the DND did not provide him with the estimates that would go along with operating the F-35, even after he asked them to do so.

"Over the past few weeks, it has become clear that the Department of National Defence provided the PBO with figures that did not include all operating costs," Page told the committee. "The PBO understood that it had been provided with full life-cycle costs from the DND as required."

After his testimony, reporters asked Page if the government had withheld the cost information deliberately from Canadians, to which Page replied, "Yes."

And there were still more problems with the actual airplane. Besides the reports of the peeling and bubbling fibre mat, there were now problems with the helmet-mounted display and its night-vision capabilities, jittery readouts and delays in transmitting data to the helmet display. There was talk of simply finishing the helmet later, after the F-35 was in service, but it was pointed out that doing so could result in an expensive retrofit of an aircraft that had just been built. There was also a lot of computer code that still needed to be verified—the program as a whole featured more than 20 million lines of code, more than 9 million lines of which were actually executed in the F-35 airplane, and each line had to be checked for errors.

The obvious problems didn't stop Lockheed Martin from putting pressure on Canada. The company said that if Canada pulled out of its MOU, Canadian companies would miss out on the chance to bid on work.

"Right now we will honour all existing contracts we have," Steve O'Bryan, vice-president of Lockheed Martin, said. "After that, all F-35 work will be directed into countries that are buying the plane."

O'Bryan said he felt the government would still purchase the F-35.

"They're committed to the F-35. They've selected it, and we haven't had any change in that position."

In September 2012, the government announced that it had hired accounting firm KPMG to conduct an assessment of the expected costs involved in purchasing and operating the F-35. The contract would pay KPMG $643,535.

Some individuals looked for a more creative way of filling Canada's fighter needs, and retired Major-General Lewis MacKenzie became an advocate for an interesting alternative. MacKenzie and the company Bourdeau Industries had actually approached the federal government with the idea of replacing the CF-18s with the ill-fated CF-105 Avro Arrow. The Avro Arrow was an institution of Canadian lore, a made-in-Canada fighter jet. Originally designed in the 1950s, it had been considered ahead of its time with its delta-wing shape, internal weapons bay, 50,000-foot ceiling and predicted Mach 2 speed. The program to design and build the Arrow had grown expensive and was seen as outdated as intercontinental ballistic missiles grew to replace manned bombers. As a result, the program was cancelled by then-Prime Minister John Diefenbaker. The cancellation was seen as a national tragedy, but according to MacKenzie, the Arrow was still a superior fighter jet that could probably be made more cheaply than the F-35.

"It's an attack aircraft. It's designed for attacking ground targets, and its stealth is most effective against short-range radar, protecting ground targets," MacKenzie said of the F-35. "What we need in Canada is something that can go to the edge of our airspace, from a sovereignty point of view, and be able to catch up with intruders."

The Arrow, Mackenzie claimed, could actually fly 20,000 feet higher than the F-35 and the total cost of building and operations would come in at $11.73 billion, well below what was forecast for the F-35.

The government rejected the proposal, saying it would cost too much money and time, and that the Arrow did not meet its specifications...whatever those were.

Even if Canada wanted to try to save money by delaying some of the upgrades to the F-35 that would no doubt take place over the aircraft's lifespan, it was unlikely to be able to do so without risking its interoperability with other NATO F-35s. The countries that purchased the F-35 got to vote on all upgrades and developments, but the countries that bought the most planes got the most votes, meaning Canada, with its 65 planes, would never be able to oppose the United States, with its estimated 2400 F-35s, if upgrades were voted on. If Canada simply chose not to conduct the upgrades, its planes would not fly as well or communicate as efficiently with other nations' F-35s. The idea of interoperability with the aircraft other countries had been a main selling point for buying the fighter in the first place.

In December 2012, KPMG came out with its estimate of the cost of buying and operating the F-35, and the price tag had climbed again. The total cost was now pegged at $45.8 billion for 12 years of design and purchase (from decision to acquire in 2010 to final delivery in 2022) plus a 30-year operational lifespan once in service. The cost per plane was now estimated at $87.4 million at peak production, which was estimated to be in five years' time. The acquisition costs for the planes was similar to the original $9 billion total, but KPMG's calculation of the operational costs was $19.9 billion, up from the $9 billion figure that the DND had been using. And sustainment costs were estimated to be $15.2 billion, compared to the DND's predicted costs of $7.3 billion.

Within months of the KPMG report, the government let slip that it was finally looking at other options. It had gone to four other companies and asked for technical information on their aircraft. Those companies were Boeing for the F/A-18 Super Hornet, as well as Dassault, European Aeronautic Defence and Space Company (now Airbus Group) and Saab. All had six weeks to provide the technical specifications for their fighters. Once the specifications had been submitted, the government would approach the companies for cost information.

The news regarding the F-35's development continued to be grim. There were now problems with the radars not functioning properly, blurry vision in the helmet display, a headrest so big that it prevented pilots from being able to shoulder check and, of all things, an inability to fly through clouds. That data was based on testing periods from the previous year, when the United States had checked to see if the F-35 was ready for pilot training; instead, the military was forced to keep all flying in the hands of experienced test pilots. Many of the problems that had been reported a year earlier still had not been repaired. One report actually stated that "aircraft limitations prohibit flying the aircraft at night or in instrument meteorological conditions, hence pilots must avoid clouds and other weathers."

Despite those problems, the F-35 was declared ready at the end of December 2012 for extended pilot training. Any further issues would have to be ironed out during training.

A DND report from Defence Research and Development Canada painted a picture of high aircraft losses once Canada acquired the F-35. The report gave only a 54 percent chance that 63 of its 65 planes would be flying by the time the last plane had been delivered. The report noted that the reason for the high loss rate was that the aircraft was brand new and losses were always higher at the beginning of a fleet's service life. The government had been loathe to contemplate budgeting for replacement aircraft because it did not want to put the acquisition price beyond the $9 billion number that had been circulating since the decision to purchase the F-35 was announced in 2010.

Other airplane manufacturers were still pressuring the government to pick their aircraft instead. In June 2013, a vice-president for Dassault went public with remarks that its Rafale met all of Canada's needs.

"We believe that the Rafale is an aircraft that meets all the Canadian requirements and in some cases exceeds them," said Yves Robin. "The Rafale meets all of them. It also has the big advantage of the Rafale already [being there]. It is existing, and it's a risk-free program at a fair price. Said contract could be filled quickly."

On April 13, 2014, it was announced that the RCAF had finished its study of the F-35 and its rivals. The Harper government stated that it had received the options analysis the previous week and would start going over it. There was no rush, however. The government had already missed its window in 2014 to buy the F-35s, so it would have to wait until at least January 2015 to place its order if it decided to go ahead with the purchase.

More numbers were bandied about. The Centre for Policy Alternatives and the Rideau Institute estimated that the current cost predictions for the F-35 could be incorrect by anywhere from $12 billion to $81 billion over 40 years, depending on a wide assortment of risks.

On June 11, the four-person panel that had been created in the wake of the Auditor General's report issued its own report to cabinet. Their review had taken 18 months. It was not an analysis of which plane the Conservatives should choose for the military, but was instead a comparison of the F-35 and its rivals. That information was then put to the government. Despite the fact that the report was supposed to be public, it was not immediately made publicly available.

The four-person panel was, however, trotted out to discuss their report. The panel included James Mitchell, a former senior government official; Keith Coulter, a former fighter pilot and the former head of the Communications Security Establishment (CSE); Phillipe Lagassé, a University of Ottawa professor who had been critical of the selection of the F-35 when it was announced in 2010; and Rod Monette, a former federal comptroller general and senior DND manager.

"The purpose of this is not [to] reach conclusions or recommendations but to satisfy ministers that the necessary rigorous analytic work has been done, and that it's been done fairly objectively," said Mitchell during the press conference. None of the panel members would express a preference for any particular aircraft, saying that the decision was now up to senior government officials and cabinet ministers.

As of the writing of this book, there were rumours circulating in the news media that the government would still select the F-35 as its fighter of choice. However, the government has not yet announced a decision nor set a timetable for that decision.

CHAPTER SEVEN

The Guergis-Jaffer Scandal

IT IS IMPORTANT to remember that politicians are human and, like any other person, regardless of their job, can make mistakes and poor decisions. They are also capable of behaving badly, but that is a part of the common stereotype of a politician. The public regularly sees elected officials, perhaps more so in the United States, but also here in Canada, as entitled individuals who often consort with less-than-reputable individuals in an effort to further their own careers. Politicians are often seen as acting above the law or at least being treated differently by it, as sentences for politicians who are found guilty of criminal offences are often seen as being less than what an unelected individual would receive.

In 2009, a series of events took place involving a Canadian cabinet minister and her once-MP husband that saw almost all of these stereotypes either play out or were at least intimated by others to have taken place. It also marked a riveting and dramatic fall from grace for a duo that was seen as being one of Ottawa's political power couples.

Helena Guergis was first elected to the House of Commons in 2004 in the Ontario constituency of Simcoe-Grey, winning by a mere 100 votes. It was not her first try at public office—she had run in the 2003 provincial election in the constituency of Trinity-Spadina, where she finished a distant third. A long-time Conservative supporter, especially at the provincial level, Guergis worked as a constituency assistant and executive assistant for PC member of Provincial Parliament (MPP) Joe Tascona. She was later employed by Minister of Education and Finance Janet Ecker in the Ontario government of Premier Mike Harris.

Guergis was re-elected in 2006, the election in which the Conservatives won a minority government over the Liberals. She was named as a parliamentary secretary to David Emerson, Minister of International Trade. In 2007, she was appointed to cabinet when she was named a Secretary of State for Foreign Affairs and International Trade and Secretary of State for Sport. There were a few minor bumps in her performance during this time—she once gave a response to accusations of detainee treatment in Afghanistan by saying there was "no evidence" to back up suggestions of detainees being mistreated. In 2008, she publicly revealed that Liberal leader Stéphane Dion was travelling to Afghanistan. Such trips are typically kept secret as a security precaution. Dion was furious and went so far as to demand that Prime Minister Stephen Harper fire her. Harper did not.

Guergis was re-elected to her seat yet again in October 2008 and was even named to cabinet again, this time as the Minister of State for the Status of Women.

One day after the election, she and fiancé Rahim Jaffer were married in an impromptu ceremony witnessed by only a half-dozen people—the pair had planned a larger wedding but decided to get married sooner rather than later. The change in plans was auspicious, as Jaffer, once a rising star in the Conservative Party as a young MP for the constituency of Edmonton-Strathcona, had lost the seat he'd held since 1997 to the NDP. Rumours circulated that he had lost out of sheer laziness in his campaign, and in fact, Jaffer had once been elected "laziest MP" in a survey conducted by the *Hill Times*. He tried to win back the Conservative nomination to contest the seat in a future election, but the party declined to offer him an extension on the nomination process.

Despite Jaffer's loss, everything for Ottawa's newest power couple seemed to be going smoothly until September 11, 2009. In the early morning hours, the Ontario Provincial Police stopped a Ford Escape travelling at high speed through the village of Palgrave, northwest of Toronto. Rahim Jaffer was driving the Escape, which turned out to be his wife's vehicle. At the time of the stop, the vehicle was travelling 93 kilometres per hour in a 50 kilometre-per-hour zone. When the police officer approached the car, she detected the odour of alcohol on Jaffer's breath. She administered a roadside screening test, which came back positive for alcohol. A search of the vehicle also yielded a bag of powder that was determined to be cocaine. The officer took Jaffer back to the OPP detachment for a breathalyzer test, which yielded a blood alcohol level of 0.08, the minimum level under the Criminal Code for a charge of impaired driving. In all, Jaffer was charged with impaired driving and possession of cocaine, and then released. His driver's licence was automatically suspended for 90 days.

Guergis promptly issued a statement.

"I take this very seriously. I love my husband. I will wait for further information before I make any comment," the statement read.

But that was not the first scandal involving Jaffer. In 2001, one of his aides called in to a Vancouver-based national radio call-in show claiming to be Jaffer. The station later confronted Jaffer and his aide about what had happened, and they admitted that the aide had pretended to be Jaffer because the MP had been unable to participate in the show. Jaffer apologized in the House for what happened, the aide resigned and Jaffer was suspended as the chair of the Advisory Committee on Small Business and Entrepreneurship and demoted to sitting in the backbenches in the House.

But Jaffer's arrest, subsequent impaired driving and possession charges turned out to be just the opening salvo in what would become a barrage of unfortunate incidents and bad news for both Jaffer and Guergis. Six months after Jaffer's arrest, Guergis found herself in the media spotlight for her behaviour at the Charlottetown airport. On February 19, Guergis and her assistant arrived late for a flight from Charlottetown to Montréal. She apparently showed up just 15 minutes before the early evening Air Canada Jazz flight was to depart. Interviews with unnamed airport and Air Canada workers revealed that Guergis had, in essence, thrown a temper tantrum about the possibility of missing her flight.

"Everybody was...trying to get her out, trying to help her. But she took it upon herself to think everyone was trying to block her at every move. She was very unprofessional, very unorganized, very rude," one employee who witnessed the episode told the *Globe and Mail*.

"She was yelling at the Jazz agent to hurry up, that [he was] wasting her time and that she had to get going because she wanted to get home [to her husband] because it's her 'effing birthday,'" the employee described. Guergis' exact words, which were later extensively reported in the media, were "Happy fucking birthday to me. I guess I'm stuck in this hellhole."

Guergis and her assistant were told they could not take their oversized bags on as carry-on and would have to check them. The pair then went to the security doors and started banging on them.

"A staffer went to the gates to tell her to just hang on because they were literally banging and kicking on the glass at the security doors," the employee said.

Guergis then ran through the metal detector, at which point it went off. She took off her boots and threw them at a security official. Guergis was heard to have said, "I'm going to be stuck in this shithole because of you."

After clearing security, the pair had to wait at the gate to get on the plane because the person manning the gate had gone to look for Guergis and her assistant. The two again started to bang on the glass at the gate. They were then allowed to board the plane, which had been delayed for them. The delay inconvenienced, according to the employee, some 40 other people who were already on board.

On February 25, Guergis issued an apology for her behaviour at the airport. The apology apparently came only after Liberal MP Wayne Easter, who represented a constituency in Prince Edward Island, received a letter about the incident.

"On February 19, I was rushing to catch a flight at the Charlottetown Airport and spoke emotionally to some staff members. Regardless of my workload and personal circumstances, it was not appropriate and I apologize to airport and Air Canada staff. It was certainly not my intention to create any additional stress for airport or Air Canada employees who already have a very difficult job," the apology read.

Guergis went on to say that she had family in PEI, and that her father had been born in Summerside.

She apparently made a few phone calls to apologize to some individuals, but not to everyone who was affected. She received a significant amount of criticism because of the episode.

"If you're going to lose your temper, you do it behind closed doors, not in public," Peter Stoffer, the NDP MP for Sackville-Eastern Shore in Nova Scotia, said. "We're all human, we all screw up and make mistakes, but hopefully she learns from this."

On March 9, Rahim Jaffer was back in court to resolve his outstanding charges. The original charges of impaired driving and cocaine possession had been dropped because the Crown prosecutor told the court there was no reasonable likelihood of obtaining a conviction. Instead, Jaffer pleaded guilty to one count of careless driving and was fined $500. Had he been found guilty of the impaired driving charge, the automatic sentence was a one-year driver's licence suspension and $1000 fine. The possible sentences of drug possession could have included a discharge of some kind, a fine, probation, jail time or a combination of those possibilities.

"I'm sorry. I know this was a serious matter. I know I should have been more careful, and I took full responsibility for my careless driving," Jaffer said outside the courtroom after he was fined. He denied ever being in possession of drugs or driving while drunk. Rumours circulated that an officer had somehow messed up when a strip-search of Jaffer was conducted.

There were instant howls that Jaffer had received special treatment. After all, charges of impaired driving are relatively simple when it comes to securing a conviction. The Ontario Attorney General, however, said that Jaffer was treated fairly.

"Everybody has to be treated equally before the law, and when the Crown makes an assessment of the case and determines that a particular resolution is appropriate, that resolution should be the one that's obtained—whether the accused happens to be somebody who is known to the public or not known to the public. We have one rule for all and you have to adhere to the law and the law has to be administered equally," said Chris Bentley.

In response to accusations, based on Jaffer's arrest and plea, that the Tories were actually soft on crime, Veterans Affairs Minister Jean-Pierre Blackburn, a fellow Conservative, said, "It's the judges who make the decisions, not the parliamentarians."

Opposition party members and members of the public demanded that more information about Jaffer's case be made public, but the Crown refused to release any information about what had happened the night of Jaffer's arrest.

"We want to know what kind of deal was made and why they didn't proceed on the evidence," said Andrew Murie, the executive director of Mothers Against Drunk Driving (MADD).

A few days after Jaffer's court appearance, it was revealed that Helena Guergis was thinking of suing Air Canada over what had happened at the airport in Charlottetown. Specifically, she was considering suing the airline because information about the incident had been leaked to the media. The news also brought new revelations that Guergis was not particularly beloved on Parliament Hill. Rumours swirled that she had a big ego, a "prickly personality" and a large sense of entitlement based on her position in cabinet. Stories circulated in the media that chauffeurs who were responsible for driving cabinet ministers around Ottawa were actually refusing to drive for her because of how difficult she could be. The turnover rate for employees in her office, even among chiefs of staff, was high. When she appeared before a parliamentary committee not long after her airport meltdown to discuss her budget, the media turned out in large numbers. A worker from the Prime Minister's Office was also in attendance, watching. Her testimony was later described as "haughty and hostile."

Guergis couldn't stay out of the news. On March 31, only a few weeks after Jaffer's court appearance, she was making headlines again. It seemed that her executive assistant was writing letters to the editors of Ontario newspapers in which she spoke glowingly of Guergis. The issue was that when she sent these letters to local newspapers, the assistant, Jessica Craven, signed the letters as Jessica Morgan, her maiden name. Craven also did not identify herself as Guergis' executive assistant. The emails were all sent from a Yahoo! account and made no mention of Craven being an employee of Parliament. They ranged in subject matter from excusing Guergis' tantrum at the airport to criticizing opponents for a lack of policy.

The *Enterprise-Bulletin*, which served Collingwood, Ontario, in Guergis' riding of Simcoe-Grey, later confronted Craven by phone. At first, according to the *Enterprise-Bulletin*, Craven tried to deflect their questions. She told them that her maiden name was Morgan but ended the interview when she was asked if she had written the letters. Craven later turned up at the paper's office to discuss the matter. She said she was merely stating her own opinion.

"I was to make sure they were separate from what I do for a living. I am a voter in Simcoe-Grey with my own opinions," Craven said. She told the paper that Guergis did not know what she was doing.

Everything to this point was only a minor inconvenience compared to the storm of scandal that was coming. In April 2010, Guergis and Jaffer were back in the news thanks to a story published by the *Toronto Star*. According to the story, in the hours before Jaffer's arrest, he had been dining with a less-than-reputable individual and a few "busty hookers" at a high-end restaurant. At that meeting, which was also attended by several other individuals, Jaffer was alleged to have told those gathered that he could get them government grants or low-interest loans thanks to his political connections. He even went so far as to distribute his member of

Parliament business card, even though he was no longer an MP.

One of the people at the dinner was Nazim Gillani, who ran a company called International Strategic Investments. Gillani was the subject of investigations by two police agencies and Revenue Canada. One investigation was looking into a $1.5-million case of wire fraud that also involved the retail business Rona. The rumoured offences included fraud and tax evasion. Gillani operated his business out of a rented million-dollar home and, according to the *Star*, kept unseemly company. Those who hung out at the home included a former CFL player once busted for steroid production and drug possession, a lawyer suspended three times for not cooperating with probes into his businesses and many young interns and others trying to become big names in the world of finance. Gillani apparently touted himself as an individual who could successfully get grants and loans from government bodies. Most often, according to the *Star*, he searched out new businesses and promised he would help them secure financing to go public. He took a fee and then delivered nothing. Several individuals he had done business with were later told that Gillani had compromising pictures of them at a local strip club, another place where Gillani liked to do business.

The *Star* also wrote that the "busty hookers" present at the dinner with Jaffer and Gillani came from a local escort agency called Cachet Ladies. Gillani was reportedly engaged to one of the escorts.

The morning after the dinner, unaware that Jaffer had been arrested on his way home, Gillani sent out an email to some of his partners and clients, describing what

Jaffer had allegedly told him. He said, "Mr. Jaffer has opened up the Prime Minister's Office to us."

Jaffer had apparently told the group at the dinner that he still had a lot of connections on Parliament Hill and could help secure government funding for their projects. He said he had "access to a green fund." At another dinner a few weeks earlier, Gillani had told a group of businessmen that his company could get them start-up financing and that Jaffer had expertise in getting "green loans" at very low interest rates. The pair was also working with a Dr. Hai Chen on something called the "China initiative"; Chen had promised he could secure government funding in China. At the dinner the night Jaffer was arrested, the trio had planned business trips to Shanghai. The bill for the dinner came to $3200. Jaffer was driven back to his wife's Ford Escape afterward.

According to the *Star*, Jaffer was arrested shortly after midnight by an officer coming off a shift at a local RIDE checkstop that had been set up in Palgrave. She then radioed for another officer to join her. That officer had searched Jaffer and found a bag of cocaine in his pocket. Jaffer allegedly told his lawyers that the cocaine was actually in the pocket of his jacket, which was hanging on the back of the driver's seat in the car. His statement created a possible conflict that might have contributed to the outcome of Jaffer's court case.

Other interesting tidbits contained in the story included the fact that Gillani had once been charged in British Columbia with carrying a handgun. On the evening that Guergis had her meltdown at the airport in Charlottetown, Jaffer and Chen had dined together to discuss their recent trip to Shanghai, and to plan another trip the following April. The paper also revealed that the Ontario Provincial Police in Caledon, who had been responsible for Jaffer's arrest, were told by Crown attorney Marie Balogh that she did not want a trial in Jaffer's case. Officers were apparently informed that a deal with Jaffer had been made "at the most senior levels" of provincial law enforcement.

Besides creating a stir nationwide over the use of the phrase "busty hookers" to describe some of Jaffer's alleged dining companions, the reaction to the story was one of outrage. The Prime Minister's Office was quick to issue a release in response to the story, saying that Jaffer had no access whatsoever to the prime minister.

"The accusation that the Prime Minister's Office has opened doors for Mr. Jaffer or his associates is false, and frankly, it's absurd," one of Harper's spokespeople said.

It was also noted that Jaffer was still using the Conservative Party logo on a personal website. An order was promptly sent to Jaffer to remove the logo from the website.

The opposition pounced on the story.

"Who was Mr. Jaffer talking to in the Conservative government? What promises did he make of access?" thundered Michael Ignatieff, leader of the Liberal Party.

But it wasn't the only bad news to come out. At the same time as the "busty hookers" story came out, CTV reported that Jaffer was actually using one of the government BlackBerrys issued to Helena Guergis, as well as a government email address assigned to his wife for his own purposes. The use of the BlackBerry was seen as a violation of House of Commons rules, but not a criminal act. It also came to light that Guergis may have made some questionable expense claims from the last election, trying to claim shoes, clothing and jogging outfits as campaign expenses from 2010.

In response to all of the allegations, Jaffer's business, Green Power Generation (GPG), issued a statement:

> *Mr. Jaffer is a valued partner of GPG. The allegations in the* Toronto Star *are inaccurate and a complete mischaracterization of the contact between Mr. Jaffer, a principal of GPG, and Mr. Nazim Gillani of International Strategic Investments (ISI). In light of the publication, GPG intends to seek legal action against the* Toronto Star.

But the most stunning news came one day later, on April 9, when Stephen Harper revealed that Helena Guergis had resigned from cabinet, an event that was quickly reported as having been forced by the prime minister. Furthermore, Harper had also taken the extraordinary step of punting her from the Conservative Party caucus. That meant that Guergis was no longer a cabinet minister and no longer a Conservative member of Parliament—she would now have to sit as an Independent. Harper also stated that part of the reason he took this step was because of information he had received on the evening of April 8. Based on that information, the prime minister had gone so far as to call in the RCMP to investigate, but he refused to say what he had been told that he felt necessitated a police investigation.

"Last night, my office became aware of serious allegations regarding the conduct of the Hon. Helena Guergis.

These allegations relate to the conduct of Ms. Guergis and do not involve any other minister, MP, senator or federal government employee. I've referred the allegations to the conflict of interest and ethics commissioner and to the RCMP," the statement read.

Harper also said that whatever Rahim Jaffer was up to, apparently it was of no concern to the government.

In her letter of resignation, Guergis tried to maintain her innocence:

> *I take responsibility for any errors I may have made, but at no time did I compromise my oath as a Member of the Privy Council. It has become apparent through baseless allegations and unfounded assertions made about my family that I need to step aside to allow for the good work of our government to continue serving Canadians.*

But for all the bad news that was suddenly coming out about Guergis and Jaffer, no one had a clue as to the exact nature of the allegations against her that warranted an RCMP investigation. It was reported on April 12 that the allegations had come from a "third party" who had come forward but with no hint as to what this third party had disclosed. The Liberals continued to hammer away at the Conservatives in Question Period over Jaffer's alleged misdeeds. They contended that what Jaffer was doing was lobbying and that he was not a member of the lobbying registry, which all lobbyists were required to register with.

"[Jaffer] advertised his connections and his ability to influence his former colleagues. But there is a thing called the Lobbying Act. It is a law. He broke that law. And he did so, all the while bragging about and peddling the influence he had with his Conservative friends and colleagues," Liberal Martha Hall Findlay said in the House.

"Suggest[ions] that the Prime Minister's Office has opened its doors to Mr. Jaffer or his associates are absolutely without basis and are false," Transport Minister John Baird replied, as the prime minister was unavailable.

The NDP continued to press for more information.

"The government has got to provide answers now so that we can put this sordid business aside and start to deal with the important issues affecting Canadians," NDP leader Jack Layton said.

The Liberals said they believed that the accusations outlined in the *Toronto Star* story were legitimate.

"Canadians are rightly outraged that well-connected Conservatives are apparently meeting with questionable businessmen claiming they had the inside track on securing government funding. These claims are made more credible by the fact that these Conservatives appear to have had privileged access to federal cabinet," said Liberal MP Anita Neville.

The Liberals then issued a request for the lobbying commissioner to investigate Rahim Jaffer's dealings with the government. They also issued a request for the commissioner to investigate Patrick Glémaud, a one-time Conservative candidate and Jaffer's partner in GPG.

Harper had also submitted a request for the ethics commissioner to investigate Guergis. But on April 13, Mary Dawson, the commissioner, announced that she was putting her investigation on hold. A statement on the commissioner's website read:

> *Based on the information the commissioner has at this time, [Mary Dawson] is not in a position to proceed with an inquiry under the Conflict of Interest Code for Members of the House of Commons or an examination under the Conflict of Interest Act, but she will continue to monitor the situation.*

The statement went on to say that the commissioner was prevented from continuing her investigation because the RCMP were involved.

More reports of alleged inappropriate use of government resources started to emerge. A report came to light in the media that Jaffer had been using Guergis' government car and chauffeur to conduct private business. That service was only for Guergis' use in her role as a cabinet minister.

"I have never used the truck for personal use nor has Rahim," Guergis said in a statement in response to the allegation.

Two days later, the man who was the "third party" came forward to tell his story. His name was John Derrick Snowdy, a private investigator. He had been hired by a client, whose name he would not share, who was unhappy about recent business dealings he'd had with Nazim Gillani. During his time investigating Gillani, Snowdy had heard Gillani boast that he had pictures on his cellphone of both Guergis and Jaffer "partying" in the presence of prostitutes and cocaine.

Snowdy had, as a result, contacted the Conservatives to warn them of possible blackmail against Jaffer and Guergis.

"I never saw Mr. Jaffer or Ms. Guergis use cocaine. Mr. Gillani made several boastful remarks. A number of his more bizarre boasts had legs," Snowdy said.

It was also revealed that Snowdy was in a bit of trouble himself, having declared bankruptcy. He was named in an $11.9-million lawsuit and had a $2-million liability to the Canada Revenue Agency.

Gillani issued a statement in response to Snowdy's allegations.

"Naz never told anyone he had photographs nor does he have photographs of Jaffer, Guergis, cocaine or partying," said Brian Kilgore, a spokesperson for Gillani.

Snowdy later elaborated on what he had done with the information he was given. He had first contacted the Liberal Party but had not received a call back. He then contacted a Conservative riding president. That got him a call from Arthur Hamilton, a Conservative Party lawyer, to whom Snowdy relayed what he had learned in his investigation.

"The information discussed was only about Mr. Gillani. My client clearly thought that the facts of the situation mattered. He has since realized that the truth was the first victim in this situation," Snowdy said.

Snowdy had relayed another concern to the Conservatives—that a list of offshore bank accounts in Belize was registered to Gillani. Gillani had apparently said that three of those offshore accounts were to hold cash for Jaffer and Guergis.

On April 15, news reports shed some light on why Guergis had reacted so emotionally at the airport in Charlottetown back in February. It was reported that she had endured two miscarriages in the past year, the second taking place when her pregnancy was four months along. Guergis had, around that time, been forced to call an ambulance to take her mother to hospital after her mother had gone into anaphylactic shock. Her mother suffered a heart attack when she arrived at the hospital.

Rumours also circulated as to the reason Jaffer's case had been dropped by the Crown. Jaffer had apparently been denied proper access to a lawyer after his arrest. Also he had allegedly been strip-searched "under indefensible pretexts." No confirmation ever surfaced of either rumour.

More allegations were unearthed of possible unethical behaviour on Guergis' part. On April 16, Guergis acknowledged that she had sent a letter to the warden and council of Simcoe County, urging them to give a man named Jim Wright the opportunity to address their council. Wright was the owner of a company involved in alternative waste management.

"As his member of Parliament, I felt it was my obligation to support his initiative," Guergis wrote.

According to the *Toronto Star*, at the time Guergis wrote the letter, Jaffer was in the middle of negotiating an important business deal to take Wright's company public. If Guergis encouraged Simcoe County to hear from a business with which her husband was involved, that could be considered a conflict of interest. Guergis felt otherwise.

"After assuring myself that my husband had absolutely no business links or financial interest in Mr. Wright's company, I wrote to the warden and council of Simcoe

County, urging that Mr. Wright be given an opportunity to discuss his alternative waste management technology," Guergis said in her statement.

It was enough to prompt the NDP to ask the federal ethics commissioner to take a look into that allegation as well. Legislation governing the conduct of MPs prevents them from using their position to influence the decision of another person in a way that would benefit the MP or a family member of that MP. Under the federal ethics commissioner's guidelines, Guergis was allowed 30 days to respond to all the issues raised before the commissioner, Mary Dawson, could investigate.

At the same time, the Committee on Government Operations and Estimates announced that it intended to hold hearings as quickly as possible into the allegations of Guergis' and Jaffer's conduct. On April 20, Guergis requested a delay in her appearance before the committee, saying she wanted to wait to find out what the RCMP and ethics commissioner were going to do about the allegations against her.

"It has not been determined what action will be taken, if any, by these organizations, but I plan to co-operate fully as I have always maintained no wrongdoing with relation to these matters," she said in her letter to the committee.

It was announced that Jaffer and his partner Glémaud would, in fact, testify. The committee was particularly interested in discussing Jaffer's alleged lobbying activities. According to federal lobbying law, individuals had to register as lobbyists if lobbying was considered to be a large part of their job—20 percent or more of their time over a six-month period.

On April 21, both Jaffer and Glémaud appeared before the committee to answer their questions. The two hours of testimony did not go well for the pair. First, Jaffer denied that he used drugs or engaged in illegal lobbying.

"I have never partaken of any illegal substance," Jaffer told the committee.

Jaffer hindered his own cause when he outright denied, in the face of questioning, the mention on his website that he was an expert in getting financial support from the Canadian government. A screen capture of his website circulated for the whole committee to read, in which Jaffer did use those words proved his denials to be spurious.

"The statement is obviously untrue. You've stated matter-of-fact one thing, and [I] now have [evidence] before me that states something different," said Conservative MP Chris Warkentin.

So Jaffer decided instead to say that the website referred to help he provided while he was a member of Parliament. After the hearing, he told reporters that the line did not refer to financial support from the government, but support in other ways.

Glémaud was a difficult witness, openly combative and defiant in his testimony. NDP member of Parliament Pat Martin summarized his impressions of Glémaud by saying, "I don't believe you as far as I can throw you."

During Jaffer's testimony, Martin asked him, "Did [Mr. Gillani] give you cocaine in terms of part of your payment for services to be rendered? What's wrong with your ethical radar that some alarms didn't go off in your head?"

"Mr. Martin, I'm disappointed you continue to allege things [for which] you have no basis in truth," Jaffer replied.

Jaffer also made a statement of apology to Guergis for what had happened to her.

"I know the error of my judgment created significant problems for her politically. She has been a good minister and a great MP for her constituents," Jaffer said.

But there was more to Jaffer's dealings with the government than just a few allegations of using a government BlackBerry and claiming he had access to the prime minister. On April 22, the Conservatives tabled documents showing that Jaffer's company had sought as much as $135 million in federal government grants or loans for three different business projects.

One of those projects involved a division of Wright Tech Systems called Green Rite Solutions. Wright Tech Systems was the company for whom Helena Guergis had written a letter to the Simcoe County Council—an interesting connection, considering the allegation the opposition was making about the letter to the ethics commissioner. Jaffer had, in fact, been looking for a $100-million government grant for Green Rite Solutions.

But Jaffer had, in his testimony the previous day, denied ever seeking government loans or grants.

"By no means do we secure government funding," Jaffer had said.

The documents now seemed to prove that Jaffer had lied. They showed that Jaffer and Glémaud had given three business plans to Brian Jean, the parliamentary secretary for Minister of Infrastructure John Baird. Of those three, two had been considered seriously before being rejected.

"It's pretty obvious to all concerned that the commodity that Mr. Jaffer's company had to sell was access [to] and influence [over] government grants. I mean, if that's not lobbying, I don't know what is. And it may even cross the line to influence peddling," Martin said.

The committee was looking forward to learning more the next week when Nazim Gillani was scheduled to testify before the committee. In a statement prior to his testimony, Gillani, through his spokesperson, let it be known what he would tell the committee.

"Mr. Gillani's understanding was that the experience of Mr. Jaffer and Mr. Glémaud meant that they could advance proposals, projects, ideas to both public servants and elected officials with the idea that if government officials thought the proposals worthy, grants and loans might be available," said spokesperson Brian Kilgore.

But before Gillani could testify, Jaffer's partner, Patrick Glémaud, decided to take a different tack. He penned a letter to the chair of the committee, member of Parliament Yasmin Ratansi, alleging that the harsh treatment he and Jaffer had endured during their testimony had been motivated by racism. Jaffer had moved to Canada from Uganda as a young boy, while Glémaud was Haitian Canadian. Glémand wrote:

> We were quite disappointed by the unprofessional and unfair treatment that we were subject to by some of the members of the committee. It was our understanding as per the invitation we received from your office that the members' questions would be regarding the scope of the study, and not a barrage of personal attacks based on unproven allegations and innuendo.

And more revelations were coming. On April 23, Environment Minister Jim Prentice revealed that Jaffer had met with one of his staffers the previous April to discuss a business idea. Prentice said he sent his information to the lobbying commissioner and ethics commissioner, as well as to the government operations committee. Martin let it be known that Jaffer might be called back to testify again.

"You can't come to a parliamentary committee with a boldfaced lie and expect there to be no consequences. We won't accept that," Martin said.

On April 26, Prentice added more information about the story he had related. He said that when meeting the aide to discuss his business idea, Jaffer had used Guergis' office. The meeting had taken place six months after he had lost his seat. When Jaffer was asked by the committee about using his wife's resources for his personal business, he replied, "I very rarely ever went in there other than to do spousal things like help her with Christmas cards, sit in on scheduling meetings, things maybe your spouse does."

Nazim Gillani appeared before the committee to offer his testimony. He told them outright that he believed Jaffer was his "Canadian government money access point."

"Mr. Jaffer seemed to state to this committee last week that we ended our relationship months ago. This was untrue," Gillani told the committee. He subsequently distributed a copy of a contract with GPG that showed the company would receive a finder's fee for helping Gillani find financing for its business, *including* federal funding. It was another mark against Jaffer because it is illegal to receive a "finder's fee" when federal government funding is involved. Despite Glémaud's assertion that his and Jaffer's company had never entered into a contract with Gillani, Gillani was able to show the committee a contract signed by both Jaffer and Glémaud.

Gillani did, however, tell the committee he had never seen Jaffer use or even speak of cocaine and had no pictures of Jaffer or Guergis in the presence of either prostitutes or cocaine.

Allegations that Jaffer had misused Guergis' government resources were given more fuel when it was revealed that Canwest News had obtained documents that showed Jaffer was using those resources to lobby for business. The lobbying commissioner had been given more than 50 pages of documents proving Jaffer had meetings and communications with many politicians and senior government officials to discuss business. Included in that evidence were copies of several emails sent from Guergis' parliamentary email address to various politicians, officials and bureaucrats between January 2009 and March 2010 that were either signed by Jaffer or contained the words, "It's Rahim here."

Included in those documents were emails sent from Guergis' account to the following:

- Member of Parliament Brian Jean, in which Jaffer and Glémaud tried to get Jean to sign off on $135 million in funds for three different projects;
- a senior aide to Tony Clement on March 17, 2010, asking for information about the government's plans to lift foreign ownership restrictions in the telecommunications sector;
- an aide to member of Parliament Diane Albonczy in September 2009, asking for a meeting for a friend who had been of help in Jaffer's political career. At the time, Albonczy was the Minister of Small Business and Tourism. Apparently no meeting was ever arranged.

The opposition was critical of this new information, saying it showed Jaffer had privileged access to members of Parliament, senior bureaucrats and other senior government officials.

"It seems that if one has good Conservative credentials and knows the secret handshake, doors open, officials jump and illegal is just a sick bird," Pat Martin told the House. "I want to know when the prime minister is going to take responsibility for his ministers running roughshod over the Federal Accountability Act, the very centrepiece legislation of the government's agenda."

The Liberals stepped up their criticism as well.

"The prime minister's [staff] assured Canadians that the government's doors were locked to Rahim Jaffer, and then we learned of one Conservative minister, then a second Conservative minister, [and finally] a seventh Conservative minister who granted privileged access to

Mr. Jaffer. Why did it take so long to make this information public? What are the Conservatives trying to hide?" asked Liberal MP Siobhàn Coady in the House of Commons.

John Baird, speaking for the government, said that the Conservatives were being ethical by providing the documentation they had.

"And we would not be having this debate about documents if it were not for the government, which made all these documents public," Baird said.

On May 3, the Liberal Party followed up its criticism by accusing Conservative cabinet ministers of violating conflict of interest guidelines when it let Jaffer pitch his ideas to people in government.

"Providing opportunities for buddies to further their private interests [and] giving preferential treatment to people based on the buddies who represent him is illegal, regardless of whether or not money changed hands," said Liberal MP Dominic LeBlanc. "[Several ministers] and others shepherded government funding applications through privileged channels all for their buddy Rahim Jaffer. The question is simple. Why can the prime minister not admit that this is illegal?"

Stephen Harper replied, "The Liberal Party gets more and more ridiculous in the reaches it makes on this question. The fact of the matter, of course, is that Mr. Jaffer received no contracts from the government. The fact of the matter is that it has been ministers and the government who have revealed virtually all of the information that is available here because it has been turned over to the lobbying commissioner. The government has acted absolutely correctly, and quite frankly, the Liberal Party can take some lessons."

The Conservatives, now taking a pounding over Rahim Jaffer and Helena Guergis, decided to take away any chance Guergis had of running again under the Conservative banner when it stripped her of her right to do so in the next election. The Conservative Party of Canada governing council had decided on May 5 to withdraw her nomination.

"This is a serious decision that the [governing council] has made, as it overrides the democratic choice of the members in the riding Simcoe-Grey with regard to my candidacy," Guergis replied, stating that she intended to appeal the decision.

On May 10, Guergis decided to take her case straight to Canadians when she sat down with Peter Mansbridge of the CBC for a highly anticipated interview that was broadcast nationally. During the interview, she re-created her answers in response to the phone call she had received from Harper telling her she was out of cabinet and out of the party.

"Can you please tell me what I have done so I can address this? I don't understand what you're talking about. What are you talking about?" Guergis said she had asked the prime minister.

"I understand that things have been difficult, you know, in the media for the last little while for lots of reasons, but I believe that it's all been blown out of proportion and I know that when you look at the truth that it's not to that extent," she told Mansbridge of her reaction. Harper referred to a lawyer, Arthur Hamilton, who had brought the allegations against her. She said that after she had finished talking to Hamilton, she still had no idea what she had done wrong.

"I feel as though they've thrown the rule book out the window. That they're not respecting due process at all. I find it very undemocratic. I'm hurt by the prime minister. I'm hurt because I did consider him a friend as well, so I find that very hard to deal with," Guergis said.

When Mansbridge asked her about the allegations of prostitutes and cocaine, she replied, "Absolutely false. Never happened. Never would happen."

Of her husband Rahim Jaffer and his use of her resources, Guergis said, "He had his own office, he has his own emails, he has his own accounts, he doesn't need [mine]. He knows what he can and cannot do, and he's not going to be foolish enough or disrespectful enough to use taxpayers' money for his own personal business."

The response from the prime minister to her interview came from his director of communications, Dimitri Soudas, who said, "She spoke to [lawyer] Arthur Hamilton, who informed her of the allegations to be forwarded to the RCMP and the ethics commissioner. The day she resigned, she issued a statement denying the allegations. If she didn't know about the allegations, what is she denying?" he said.

On May 12, John Snowdy, the private investigator whose allegations had led to Guergis' dismissal from cabinet and caucus, appeared to testify for the committee looking into the affair. He made no secret of the contempt he felt for what had transpired since he'd had contact the Conservative Party.

"There is way too much being made of this issue when, in the first place, it appears it has been effectively dealt with by the prime minister," Snowdy said.

Snowdy still wouldn't name the client who had hired him, but he did provide a little more detail into what he had been doing. He said that he had posed as an investor interested in signing a deal with Gillani in order to get close to him. During one discussion, Snowdy said, Gillani boasted of how he could secure federal funding through Rahim Jaffer. When Snowdy asked how that was possible, Gillani waved his phone at him and suggested that he had pictures of Jaffer and Guergis in the presence of cocaine users and prostitutes. Snowdy said he never actually saw the pictures.

When asked by the committee if Gillani was the kind of person who would blackmail Guergis and Jaffer, he replied "Without a doubt."

Snowdy said that he and his client felt they had a duty to inform the party of what they had learned. He added that Guergis and Jaffer had dined with Gillani, but it had been for social reasons.

"When the Minister for the Status of Women is dining in a restaurant with a man accused of serious crimes, it's about the optics...you tell me how the Hill here would have responded to it," Snowdy said.

Snowdy also told the committee that he had been shown a list of offshore companies in Belize. When he asked Gillani if he could use three of the companies on the list, Gillani had replied that those three were reserved for Rahim Jaffer and Helena Guergis.

As soon as Snowdy had finished testifying, Gillani, through his spokesperson, issued a statement.

"Mr. Snowdy has taken full advantage of immunity afforded by the House of Commons committee hearing to offer a mix of innuendo, political attacks against the [Liberal] party, misinformation, insults to the committee and to me, and only a few facts that add a veneer of credibility," the statement said.

Meanwhile, Commissioner Mary Dawson's investigation of Helena Guergis was moving along, and although she didn't have any evidence relating to the larger issue of Guergis' and Jaffer's conduct, she did, on May 20, find that Guergis had committed one violation. According to Dawson, Guergis had failed to report a mortgage on her new Ottawa home. Public office holders were required to report liabilities of more than $10,000. In the previous year, Guergis had purchased an $890,000 home. The loan against the home was from Scotiabank, and Guergis had not declared it. She was fined $100.

Guergis finally confronted the prime minister about the allegations against her from her new spot as an Independent member of Parliament, rising in the House of Commons to ask him to reveal those allegations and to make public the letter he had sent to the ethics commissioner. Snowdy had recently claimed that what he had said was misrepresented in the letter.

But any hope the public had of hearing more from Guergis in committee testimony was quashed on June 7 when she said that an illness would prevent her from appearing. The following day, Jaffer also did not appear for another round of testimony.

"This is his decision and his alone—and we are pissed. Now we use the summons. I don't care if we have to drag him here in the back of a paddy wagon," said Pat Martin.

On June 9, Arthur Hamilton appeared before the committee and was finally able to make public more of the allegations against Guergis. In his testimony, he said that the reason Guergis was fired was because the party had been told that she was helping Jaffer in a business scheme to defraud investors. He stated that he'd told Guergis over the phone the night she was fired what the allegations against her were.

"The basis of [Mr. Snowdy's] allegations was…there is a significant attempt by Mr. Gillani and Mr. Jaffer to defraud potential investors as they hold themselves out to be venture capitalists. That's the base. Mr. Snowdy advised that Ms. Guergis was assisting Mr. Jaffer in this enterprise," Hamilton said.

He told the committee that Guergis was there to lend credibility to Jaffer's scheme.

"Mr. Jaffer was creating the illusion that he was ultra-connected with the Conservative government and that he could make funds available and effectively open doors to potential investors. Ms. Guergis assisted and amplified that aura of connectedness," Hamilton said. He added that he had other sources of information besides what Snowdy had told him.

The committee again issued a summons for Jaffer to appear on June 16, but he again ignored them. Jaffer later issued a statement in which he said he had missed the appearance because he had been at a doctor's appointment with his wife regarding their pregnancy.

He did, however, appear the following day and made no secret of how he felt about both the hearing and the Conservative Party.

"I think many things have happened since the 2008 election that lead me to believe...that the Conservative Party of today is not the same party that I worked so hard to develop," Jaffer said.

The committee tried to question Jaffer about the discrepancies between his testimony and information the committee had since learned of, but Jaffer wouldn't co-operate, even when the committee mused that Jaffer might be in contempt of Parliament. They pointed out that he might have misled the committee and that the documentation the committee had requested a month ago had not yet been provided to them. Jaffer's appearance, however, yielded little new information.

A month later, the RCMP finally reported back regarding their investigation into the matter, as requested by the prime minister. They said they would not be laying any charges against either Helena Guergis or Rahim Jaffer. Despite the RCMP's findings, however, the Conservatives were not willing to take her back.

"The RCMP's decision will not affect Ms. Guergis' removal from cabinet or caucus," said PM spokesperson Sarah MacIntyre. "There were several factors that led to Ms. Guergis' removal from cabinet and caucus, and the ethics commissioner is still conducting an investigation into her actions."

Rahim Jaffer released a statement through lawyer Frank Addario that stated, "It has been determined that there is no evidence to support a criminal charge and it will be closing the portion of its file that relates to Mr. Jaffer."

Yet despite the proclamation that there would be no charges, the RCMP would not provide any additional detail as to the exact nature of the allegations. Even members of the opposition were sympathetic to Guergis.

"For all appearance, the prime minister overreacted based on the flimsiest of accusations, and he ruined Helena Guergis' career. I think he owes us an explanation as to what offence was so unforgiveable and so heinous to kick her not only out of cabinet, but right out of the party, and making her virtually unemployable. At the very least, he owes Helena Guergis an apology," Pat Martin said. He added that she probably had a good case for a lawsuit, if she chose to pursue one.

But Guergis was more concerned with trying to get back in with the Conservative Party. The day after the RCMP's announcement, Guergis called for a meeting with Stephen Harper.

"I think it's time for a face-to-face meeting between the prime minister and I. He can raise his concerns, whatever they are, and I can answer. I have never been afforded this opportunity," she said. But no such meeting was ever held.

Guergis wasn't the only person cleared of criminal charges. It was announced that wire fraud charges against Gillani had also been dropped.

On August 12, Guergis was back in the news when she was involved in a two-car accident at CFB Borden. The crash was notable because of the fact that Guergis was pregnant and had previously had two miscarriages. She and her assistant, who was driving the car, were taken to hospital for observation before being discharged in good health. On December 15, she gave birth to a boy, who was named Zavier Rahim Nizarali.

On March 26, 2011, coming up on the one-year anniversary of her ousting from the cabinet and caucus, and with a federal election just announced because the Harper government had fallen in the House of Commons, Guergis sat down for an interview. She agreed when it was suggested she had faced something of a double standard, when it was revealed that other MPs facing criminal charges had not been punished as severely as she had.

"We all know that there were so many lies spread around about me, and it's been really difficult to come out of what happened last year. But I'm stronger and I'm wiser. I also want to say that I would never, ever wish upon anyone what has happened to me. I think that leadership is about embracing dissent. I think leadership is about recognizing mistakes you've made and then taking the steps to rectify them. I don't think [Stephen Harper] has done that," she said.

She added that she had lost a lot of respect for the prime minister.

"There was a time when I would do anything [Stephen Harper] asked of me. They used me to their advantage. But now, all of a sudden, I'm not a benefit according to him, so he cuts me loose."

She said she felt that Harper was still a barrier to her joining caucus again, saying several party members had been supportive of her return. She also said that what happened to her could cause more women to think twice about a career in politics.

"I think there are a lot of women who are disheartened about how I've been treated in politics. I think that most of all, though, they're just completely disgusted at the way politicians behave. My pitch is that there should be more Independents. That way, you don't always have to tow the party line, be on the attack and spew the rhetoric. I don't have to have anything approved or vetted. I can speak my mind freely."

Guergis had already announced her intention to run as an Independent in Simcoe-Grey because the Conservatives had already filled her nomination. On April 15, she called a news conference to say that she had finally obtained, through an Access to Information request, a copy of the RCMP report against her. Among the more stunning allegations was the claim that there was a video of her "snorting cocaine off the breasts of a prostitute."

"The details of this report are extremely disturbing. It has demonstrated that there was a concerted effort to perpetrate lies and smear my good name. If only Mr. Harper had taken the time to be open about the allegations that were presented to him, and had given me a chance to confront them, much hardship could have been avoided," Guergis said.

She cried at times during the news conference as she discussed the ordeal, saying, "The damage is real, it is deep and it is permanent. Imagine waking up every day for months seeing headlines and stories that have no basis in reality, attacking your credibility and everything you have worked so hard for, and having to face the public under this unfair scrutiny and pressure."

When asked about Guergis on the campaign trail, Harper replied that she would not be invited back.

"There were, as you know well, a range of political problems around this individual. They have been discussed among members of our caucus. There is simply no desire to see the return of this individual to our caucus," Harper said.

When the results of the election were announced on May 2, Stephen Harper had won a majority government. But Helena Guergis would not be returning as a member of Parliament; she lost to Kellie Leitch, the Conservative who was nominated to replace her. Guergis, in fact, finished third, also coming in behind the NDP challenger, Katy Austin.

Two months after that loss, the ethics commissioner finally reported back on her investigation into Guergis. Mary Dawson said that Guergis had, in fact, acted unethically and violated the code of ethics when she had sent the letter to the Simcoe County Council about Jim Wright and his waste management company. She found that Rahim Jaffer was connected to the company at the time the letter was sent. She also said she had found "substantial inconsistencies and gaps in the testimony of important witnesses."

She concluded that Jaffer had a private interest in relation to the letter because he expected to benefit financially from the work he did with Wright and his business.

Specifically, Dawson found that Guergis had breached Sections 8 and 9 of the Conflict of Interest Code for Members of Parliament. Section 8 prohibits MPs from acting in their own interest or that of their family, whereas Section 9 bans MPs from using their position to influence decisions from which they or their family could benefit.

Just before Christmas, Guergis decided to take Pat Martin's advice, and she filed a lawsuit over how she had been treated by Harper and the Conservatives. The lawsuit named Stephen Harper, the Conservative Party and several others, and sought compensation in the amount of $1.3 million. In her lawsuit, Guergis stated that she was suing the prime minister for "conspiracy, defamation, misfeasance in public office, intentional infliction of mental suffering and negligence."

The Prime Minister's Office replied that it did not agree with the allegations in the lawsuit.

"The allegations are groundless, and they will be refuted vigorously. This latest action is ridiculous. The voters have made their minds up about Helena Guergis," said press secretary Carl Vallee.

Besides the prime minister and the party, Guergis was suing two of the prime minister's senior aides; Arthur Hamilton, the Conservative Party lawyer who had told her of the allegations against her; and two Conservative members of Parliament.

"The conspiracy was to engage in unlawful acts in order to remove and/or justify the removal of the plaintiff from her positions as a member of the caucus of CPC (Conservative Party of Canada), the candidate for the CPC in the Electoral District of Simcoe-Grey and the Minister of State for the Status of Women, in a manner deemed by the defendants to be to their political, personal and/or financial benefit," the lawsuit read. It also stated that "the defendants engaged in arbitrary, reckless, capricious, malicious, high-handed and arrogant conduct."

Specifically, Guergis was seeking general damages of $800,000, another $250,000 in aggravated damages and $250,000 in punitive damages. In August 2012, Ontario Superior Court Justice Charles Hackland dismissed Guergis' lawsuit. That same year, Guergis moved to Edmonton where she began studying law at the University of Alberta.

Guergis filed an amended statement of claim in 2013, specifically against John Snowdy, the private investigator, Conservative member of Parliament Shelly Glover, a lawyer who had represented Stephen Harper in the original lawsuit and that lawyer's law firm. Hackland ruled that this lawsuit was an abuse of process and dismissed it, too. Guergis was left with $33,000 in court costs from the first lawsuit and $118,560 from the second. The Conservatives tried to have any further action blocked until such time as she repaid those costs. She was allowed to pay them back at the rate of $30 per month—she had argued that she was now a university student and that amount was all she could afford. At that rate, the media calculated, it would take her 347 years to pay off those costs.

Guergis filed a third lawsuit on June 20, 2014, this one seeking $4 million in damages. She was specifically seeking $2.25 million from Arthur Hamilton and his law firm, claiming that Hamilton had breached solicitor-client privilege with her. She is also seeking

$1.75 million from Shelly Glover, claiming that Glover defamed her in May 2010 when she was quoted as saying, of Guergis' troubles, "I can assure you there is far more to come out."

The allegations in this latest lawsuit have not yet been proven in court.

CHAPTER EIGHT

Robocalls Scandal

IN A DEMOCRACY, the right to vote is considered fundamental, so much so that many governments have laws criminalizing anything that interferes with an elector's right to cast a vote in an election. Voter fraud, while it pops up here and there in Canada, has never been systemic. But, in 2012, roughly nine months after the Conservatives won their majority government, allegations started to emerge that there might have been a concerted effort to keep non-Conservative supporters from voting in the election.

The battleground for what became known as the "robocalls scandal" was Guelph, Ontario, but in the first few weeks, it looked as if there could be as many as 18 ridings in which there was a deliberate effort to keep some Canadians from voting. The public first learned of the scandal in February 2012 when the media reported that Elections Canada was investigating reports of fraudulent phone calls made during the last election. Specifically, Elections Canada had received complaints about phone calls that some voters in Guelph had received on election day, May 2, 2011. Those phone calls were automated, and a female voice spoke to those who answered, telling them that their polling station had been moved. This led to confusion at polling stations, and the result, the media intimated, might be that some voters simply gave up and went home instead of voting.

But it wasn't just Guelph that may have been affected. In the beginning, Elections Canada also received complaints from 18 ridings across the country where voters received either deceptive automated calls telling them that their polling station had been moved, or they received live phone calls from individuals that were of a harassing or rude nature. Those live calls usually had a caller identify him- or herself as calling on behalf of a Liberal candidate.

The automated calls, according to an investigation by Postmedia News and the *Ottawa Citizen*, were traced to an Edmonton call centre called RackNine. That company had done work for both the national campaign and nine other Conservative candidates, including for Prime Minister Stephen Harper in his own constituency. Its services allowed anyone with an account to record an outgoing message, upload a list of phone numbers and send out calls. RackNine replied to the allegations that it did not know that its services had been used to make bogus phone calls. At first, the Conservatives were even reluctant to say how much work RackNine had done for them.

A common feature emerged for many of the calls that were being investigated—the phone number that showed up on the call displays of some individuals who had received calls. Investigators for Elections Canada traced that phone number to a disposable or prepaid cellphone—often referred to as a "burner" phone. That phone had a 450 area code located in the city of Joliette, Québec, northeast of Montréal. The problem with prepaid phones is that there are no billing records for them because individuals "buy" minutes for the phone in blocks, usually from any number of stores, so it is difficult to trace a burner phone to a specific name. But, by looking through RackNine server logs and other documentation from the company, Elections Canada identified an individual who might have sent out the calls.

"We couldn't possibly have known that it was RackNine that was the initiator of fake calls. I had no idea what the content of the calls were," said Matt Meier, owner of RackNine.

The bulk of the complaints seemed to be coming from Guelph. In those cases, people received automated phone calls. The voice on the line was female and spoke in both French and English. The automated call told the listener that their polling station had been changed to a mall in the downtown, where there was very little parking.

One person who received a phone call was Sue Campbell, a United Church minister whose husband John Lawson represented the Green Party in Guelph. She had already voted and returned home when she received the phone call.

"At first I thought, 'Oh that's strange.' Upon reflection, I thought, 'This can't be right. Why on Earth would it change on the day of the election?'" Campbell wondered. She wrote down the number from her caller ID and called Elections Canada to complain.

But Campbell wasn't the first. Documents obtained by the media showed that emails were already flying around on election day about calls telling voters to go to a different polling station. As more and more calls came in, election officials in Guelph decided they had to do something to help people who might actually go to the shopping centre downtown, expecting to vote. They dispatched a worker with maps of all the different polling locations to the mall in order to intercept people sent there. Within one hour, more than 100 people had come to the mall expecting to vote. The media were also enlisted to help, with messages going out over radio stations warning people in Guelph about the phone calls.

But the calls didn't just happen in Guelph. Similar calls were reported in the ridings of Kitchener-Waterloo, Kitchener-Conestoga, London-West, Parkdale-High Park, Winnipeg South Centre and Sydney-Victoria.

Postmedia and the *Ottawa Citizen* had also obtained phone bills showing that a phone call came from the Guelph campaign office for Conservative candidate Marty Burke to Matt Meier's cellphone shortly after 11:00 AM. Another call was placed to RackNine's main number shortly after 7:00 PM. They also learned that Andrew Prescott, a volunteer with Burke's campaign, had used RackNine to send out another automated call warning about the bogus phone calls.

"I was not involved in the illegal phone calls. I am a legitimate user of RackNine's services and have been for several years. I am a devoted believer in free and fair elections. I would never partake in *any* illegal activities and openly advocate for everyone to play by the rules," Prescott wrote in an email.

The impact of the calls was questionable; Liberal MP Frank Valeriote still won his seat by more than 6000 votes. When the media contacted Burke for comment, he referred them to his former director of communications, Michael Sona. Sona was now working for Conservative MP Eve Adams and did not initially return media calls.

The Conservatives were quick to deny any knowledge of the calls.

"The Conservative Party of Canada ran a clean and ethical campaign and would never tolerate such activity," said campaign manager Jenni Byrne. "The party was not involved with these calls and if anyone on a local campaign was involved, they will not play a role in a future campaign."

When questioned in the House of Commons, Prime Minister Stephen Harper replied, "In this case, our party has no knowledge of these calls. It's not a part of our campaign."

People were also starting to complain of other calls that featured a live caller, often claiming to be from the Liberal Party. The calls were made repeatedly, often late at night or early in the morning. Some of the calls contacted Jewish families at mealtimes on Saturdays, the Sabbath, upsetting them. Others reported that the person on the other end of the phone mimicked certain accents in a disrespectful way. Liberal campaign offices began receiving phone calls from residents, wondering when they were going to receive the lawn sign they'd ordered. All the calls seemed to be made in constituencies where the Conservatives were in a tight race with the Liberals, but they did not take place in every riding where the race was seen as being close.

Even constituency offices for Liberal candidates received such calls. The calls often came from a North Dakota number—701-590-8703. An Internet search revealed many listings in message boards where the number was said to be associated with fraudulent credit card schemes.

Making such calls, whether live calls or recorded robocalls, was not difficult because all parties kept lists of known supporters and also of people known to support other parties. The Conservatives had a large database called the Constituent Information Management System (CIMS) that housed all such information. It was relatively straightforward for other campaigns to get access to those records.

The Liberals were starting to think the robocalls were part of a larger conspiracy, an effort to suppress the vote in certain constituencies. The Conservatives were quick to deny the allegation, however, saying their national campaign chairman, Guy Giorno, would never allow such actions to take place.

"The only party with access to the Liberal Party member list is the Liberal Party. Are you certain they aren't making the calls to their members?" said Conservative Party spokesperson Alykhan Velshi, when asked about what was happening.

The harassing, live calls were reported in several different ridings, including Oakville, Ontario, where callers spoke with a person who faked an accent similar to that of the candidate; Hadimand-Norfolk, Ontario, where early morning calls were waking people up; St. Paul's in Toronto, where Jewish voters complained of repeated calls on the Sabbath; Parkdale-High Park in Toronto, where calls were made late at night; Saint Boniface, Manitoba, where voters complained of early morning phone calls; and Niagara Falls, Ontario, where voters complained of late-night phone calls.

With respect to the robocalls, the media were still hoping to talk Michael Sona. But now news came out that he had left his job with Eve Adams' office, and rumours were brewing that he might have had a role in the automated calls. The opposition accused the Conservatives of trying to blame the entire scandal on one person. But Sona still had not made any comment to the media.

By February 26, 2012, the number of ridings that had received calls about changed polling stations was now up to 34. Interim Liberal leader Bob Rae was critical.

"What inevitably happens is that people will look back at what they thought was an isolated incident in their riding, and then they begin to understand that it may have been part of some sort of larger pattern," said Rae. He said he believed that in as many as 27 of those ridings, the phone calls had affected the outcome.

Under election law, it is illegal to try to prevent someone from voting. Doing so can be punishable by either a $5000 fine or a five-year prison term or both.

The Elections Canada investigator tasked with looking into the allegations was Al Matthews, a former fraud investigator with the RCMP. He was granted an order compelling RackNine to turn over documentation, including emails, billing records and other correspondence between it and the Conservative campaign in Guelph, as well as the user names, passwords and IP addresses of anyone in Guelph who had used RackNine between March 26 and 31, 2011. He also wanted all records for calls that used the 450 number belonging to the burner cellphone.

Within days, the media had a name for the individual who owned the cellphone. It was immediately apparent that it was an alias. The name was Pierre Poutine, and the address listed for Poutine in Joliette was on Separatist Street. The name and the fact that the burner phone operated with Virgin Mobile came from documents that Matthews had filed with the courthouse. The documents also showed that the phone belonging to Pierre Poutine had been activated on April 30, 2011, only two days before the election. At first the phone was used to call only two numbers other than its own voicemail, and both those numbers were associated with RackNine. On the day before the election, the RackNine number was called from the burner phone seven times from somewhere in Guelph.

Pat Martin of the NDP quickly noted that the people who typically used burner cellphones were not upstanding citizens.

"Who uses a burner cellphone? Dope dealers and Hell's Angels and Tony Soprano use burner phones," Martin observed.

The scope of the investigation was growing—as many as 50 ridings were being investigated. On March 4, Conservative campaign chair Guy Giorno finally spoke on the issue.

"Our focus was on persuading people to vote for the Conservative Party, mobilizing that vote to turn up at the polls—those were the primary and, in fact, the only objectives in our campaign," Giorno said.

He denied that the Conservatives took part in any kind of robocall or live call campaigns to suppress votes. Rumours even circulated that Giorno had been so concerned with following the rules in the campaign that he had hired one person whose sole full-time job was to ensure the party was following campaign and election law.

"If you're running a good campaign, you don't have time for any shenanigans outside those three core activities of identification, persuasion and mobilization," Giorno said. He also called on the authorities to get to the bottom of the matter.

"We're as concerned as anybody. Not just me, not just the prime minister—the tens of thousands of Conservative volunteers who worked hard to bring a majority victory, working in an ethical, law-abiding way," Giorno said.

Some in the Conservative Party believed that it might have been Elections Canada itself that was responsible for the robocalls. Even as the number of complaints nationwide reached 31,000, Maurice Vellacott, a Conservative MP, said he thought Elections Canada had a role to play in the scandal.

"I suspect that, at the end of the day, if Elections Canada has the resources to do a proper investigation, they'll find themselves significantly responsible, that tech issues with marrying [Elections Canada] lists to available, electronic phone lists is part of the problem, and in a few instances, there may have been malfeasance by one party or another," Vellacott said.

Many believed that the Conservative Party already had a good idea who was responsible for the calls. A column in the *National Post* pointed to the Conservative's CIMS and noted that individuals with access needed to log on to retrieve whatever information they were looking for. The Conservatives, the paper said, should have easily been able to check their records to see who logged on to CIMS when, and what they actually downloaded.

"You can't do a transaction in CIMS without it being logged. The party will know who was doing what, how long they were on for and what information they were looking for. It's a difficult system do something illegal on. It's jealously guarded information," a source told the paper.

The owner of RackNine was also closing in on a potential suspect, and in doing so had found a second alias that Pierre Poutine had used. Meier found a Rogers IP address that had been used to send out the robocalls. With that knowledge, Elections Canada could approach Rogers with an order to produce the name of the person who used that IP address.

Meier said that someone named Pierre Jones had contacted him during the election. Jones had told Meier that he was a bachelor of commerce student studying advertising at the University of Ottawa and wanted to learn more about call centres. In setting up an account, Jones gave Meier a false address in Joliette, 54 Lajoie Nord, which was at least slightly more plausible than Separatist Street. The emails came from an untraceable email address at pierres1630@gmail.com. In paying for the RackNine services, Jones used a PayPal account, which was attached to a prepaid Visa gift card, again making the transaction untraceable. During the campaign, Jones set up several different calls, but only one was sent out. It wasn't until Meier was served with the production order from Elections Canada that he started digging through his records to find out who had used them for the robocalls. He found Jones' account in the system and started to look at every interaction Jones had with RackNine's system. For almost all of his interactions, Jones had accessed RackNine using a proxy server to hide his tracks, but Meier found one instance in which Jones did not do so, and was able to find the IP address he had used.

"He [Pierre Jones] screwed up. Just for a fraction of a second, but it was enough for me to find him," Meier said.

The fact that someone had used RackNine for possibly illegal purposes had motivated Meier to track down the perpetrator.

"I was shocked the moment Matthews explained some party had used RackNine's service in an attempt to disrupt voting in the 2011 election. Our dialling services have been used successfully by hundreds of campaigns to engage voters and inform them of where and when to vote in many elections. The fact our software was used even once for something like this is devastating, and we're working tirelessly to correct that," said Meier.

More evidence was coming out about the scope of the phone calls. On March 16, it was revealed that the deceptive robocall Pierre Poutine sent out had reached 5053 people just within the 519 area code. That area code included Guelph, Kitchener-Waterloo, London, Windsor and Sarnia in Ontario. But others in Ontario received phone calls as well: 35 people in Toronto were called; 74 in the suburban area around the Greater Toronto Area; 14 in the 613 area code that includes Kingston and Ottawa; 22 in the 705 area code that includes Barrie, Sudbury and North Bay; and one person in Thunder Bay. A few other reports emerged, however, of such calls being made outside Ontario. That seemed to indicate the scandal as a whole was likely limited to Ontario.

A Conservative source informed the media that given the kinds of people who had received calls, predominately Liberal supporters, it seemed to indicate that whoever had accessed the CIMS database to get the information had downloaded the party's list of people who did not support the Conservative Party. That list also contained many errors because it was not maintained as rigorously as the supporter list. This explained why some places such as Liberal Party campaign offices had received phone calls.

Marty Burke, the Conservative candidate for Guelph, still said he had no idea what had happened. His wife spoke on his behalf.

"We have no idea what happened and we'd like to know, just like anybody else. We are hoping Elections Canada completes their investigation and finds whoever did this," said Patricia Burke.

On March 28, Marc Mayrand, the chief electoral officer, testified on the issue of the robocalls before the Standing Committee on Procedure and House Affairs.

"These are very serious matters that strike at the integrity of our democracy. Whether it was organized or bigger or whatever, the fact that electors, at least that we know in Guelph, were misdirected by calls falsely made on behalf of Elections Canada is absolutely outrageous," Mayrand said.

He called for Parliament to have stiffer penalties for violating provisions of the Elections Act.

"It should be sanctioned severely and we need to look at the legislation to see if we have the right framework in a modern democracy," Mayrand says.

Mayrand said that Elections Canada had now received 800 phone calls about specific incidents of improper or deceptive phone calls. Those calls all came from people in about 200 ridings, in 10 different provinces and one territory. A total of 40,000 people had contacted Elections Canada to express their concern on the issue. He further explained that William Corbett, the commissioner of Canada Elections, was working on 250 files, but any one file could contain multiple complaints. He stated that approximately 6700 phone calls had been made from the Pierre Poutine RackNine account but that only 70 complaints had been received as a result of those calls. He did say there was reason to believe that some voters had been misdirected.

On May 4, news came that Meier had isolated an IP address when he combed through Pierre Poutine/Jones' account. The IP address was used by Marty Burke's campaign office and had actually been used by Andrew Prescott when he uploaded legitimate calls to RackNine. That same IP address was used to make the Pierre Poutine calls. There was, however, no indication that Prescott was Pierre Poutine. Prescott had downloaded a list of numbers from CIMS on April 30, the same day that the Poutine burner phone had been purchased. Matthews interviewed Prescott once in February. A second interview had been scheduled but was cancelled by Prescott's lawyer.

All this information was contained in court documents filed by Matthews, but other excerpts from these documents showed investigators were closing in on a suspect. Included in the documentation were excerpts and paraphrases of interviews with other individuals that implicated Michael Sona. Matthews had interviewed a Matthew McBain, who said Sona had spoken of making misdirecting calls.

"Sona spoke to [Matthew] McBain about a campaign of disinformation such as making a misleading poll-moving call. McBain warned Sona off such conduct as the party would not stand for it," Matthews wrote in his statement.

Matthews also interviewed Chris Crawford, who had worked on the Guelph campaign. Crawford spoke of overhearing a conversation between Sona and campaign manager Ken Morgan in which Sona had been heard talking of "how Americans do politics," referring to calling non-supporters late at night pretending to be Liberals or telling voters that polls had been moved. Rumours were also circulating that Jenni Byrne, the national campaign manager for the party, had given the order to get rid of Sona when he was employed by Eve Adams.

Some groups had already started seeking legal action in response to the reports of robocalls. The Council of Canadians, a national advocacy group, filed lawsuits on behalf of individual voters seeking to have the results in seven ridings overturned owing to the robocalls scandal. Specifically, the lawsuit stated that Conservatives had engaged in "practices that if proven, point to a campaign of activities that would seek to deny eligible voters their rights to vote and/or manipulate or interfere with that right being exercised freely."

The Conservatives responded that the Council of Canadians was involved "for the improper motive of attacking only Conservatives, consistent with their vocal opposition of and malice towards the Conservative Party of Canada." The Conservatives also contended that the Council was using the lawsuits for publicity purposes to try to raise more money. On June 19, the court ruled that the lawsuits could proceed.

"Far from being frivolous or vexatious, or an obvious abuse, the application raises serious issues about the integrity of the democratic process in Canada," wrote Judge Martha Milczynski.

In August, the CRTC stepped in and started handing out fines, but did not yet deal with the robocalls scandal. Instead, the CRTC actually fined the Liberal candidate in Guelph, Frank Valeriote, for a robocall he had made during the campaign. In that robocall, voters had been told of Burke's position on abortion, but the call had not said who was responsible for the call or given a callback number. Valeriote's campaign was fined $4900 for the infraction.

On October 31, Michael Sona finally spoke up. He sat down for a broadcast interview for the CBC program *Power and Politics*. In the interview Sona, now 24, said he wasn't about to take the fall for the scandal.

"All the anonymous sources in the world can point the finger at me, but I'm not going to take responsibility for something that I'm not responsible for," Sona said "I think that there's some people that maybe had an interest in seeing me take the fall for it."

Sona said he didn't even have access to CIMS to download the list of phone numbers that would have been used.

"You've got to take a look at the options and just say, you know what, what is the more realistic option here? That some then-22-year-old guy managed to co-ordinate this entire massive scheme when he didn't even have access to the data to be able to do this, or the alternative—that this was much more co-ordinated or possibly that there were people that knew how to do this, that it was being done," Sona said.

After Sona's interview, the news in the robocalls scandal came in bits here and there. In November, it was revealed that Elections Canada had actually confronted the Conservatives three days before the election about suspicious calls that were directing voters to incorrect polling stations, but the Conservatives denied any wrongdoing. They said that some polling stations had, in fact, been changed during the campaign, and they were simply making sure voters knew about it.

On April 2, 2013, Elections Canada formally charged Michael Sona in the robocalls scandal. Specifically, he was charged with "wilfully preventing or endeavouring to prevent an elector from voting at an election." He continued to proclaim his innocence, this time speaking through his lawyer, Norm Boxall.

"I cannot help but comment, that if the government was interested in the public being fully informed and the issue of robocalls being properly addressed, a full public inquiry would be called, rather than a charge laid against a single individual who held a junior position on a single campaign and who clearly lacked the resources and access to the data required to make the robocalls. I am confident the public agrees," Boxall said. Sona's trial was scheduled for the following June.

But before the trial could take place, other legal proceedings needed to be resolved. The judge in the lawsuit brought by the Council of Canadians issued his verdict. Although he did agree that a fraud of some kind had taken place, and also that deceptive phone calls were made, Judge Richard Mosley indicated there was no evidence that anyone in the Conservative Party knew about the scheme or aided in it. Mosley, however, let it be known he was less than impressed with the behaviour of the two parties involved in the case:

> *These proceedings have had partisan overtones from the outset. That was particularly evident in the submission of the respondent [Tory] MPs [who] engaged in trench warfare in an effort to prevent this case from ever coming to a hearing on its merits.*

He reserved particular criticism for the Conservative Party:

> *Despite the obvious public interest in getting to the bottom of the allegations, the [Conservative Party of Canada] made little effort to assist with the investigation at the outset despite early requests. The record indicates that the stance taken by the respondent MPs from the outset was to block these proceedings by any means.*

Afterwards, little news on the topic came out until November 2013, when a judge lifted a public ban on the names of witnesses who would testify at Sona's trial. The witness seen as having the most damaging evidence was Rebecca Docksteader, who worked for Conservative MPs Chris Warkentin and Rob Bruinooge.

In her statement, Docksteader stated that Sona told her and another colleague that he had paid cash for a cellphone and a Visa gift card, then "recorded a message impersonating Elections Canada. Docksteader's evidence was considered to be the most damaging to Sona.

The remaining witnesses on the list were all employees of either MPs or senators. John Schudlo had also worked for Warkentin. Mitchell Messon worked for MPs Rob Moore and Steven Fletcher and Conservative Senator Carolyn Steward Olsen. Conrad John had worked for Senator Doug Finley, who had since died. Tyler Barker had also worked for Stewart Olsen, and Benjamin Hicks had been working for the Prime Minister's Office but had since left.

More information came out in April about exactly what Andrew Prescott had told investigators and would likely tell the court during the trial. Prescott had reached an immunity deal with the Crown and had said that not only Sona, but also Burke campaign manager Ken Morgan was involved. Prescott told investigators that Morgan had asked him to log into a robocall account on his computer. Later, on election day, he said that Sona had come running into a room saying, "It's working, it's working."

It was also revealed that a volunteer named John White had downloaded the list used for the phone calls, but he couldn't remember why he had downloaded it. Another document indicated that Prescott had told Matthews that Morgan and Sona had emailed him asking for contact information for RackNine. The document also showed that three-and-a-half hours after Prescott emailed Morgan and Sona the contact information, someone named Pierre Jones emailed RackNine about the account used for the calls on May 2.

Sona was openly critical of any evidence against him. He had already once provided documentation proving he was in Aruba at the time someone had supposedly told Matthews he was in Ottawa boasting about his involvement in the scandal.

"I wouldn't want to be [Prescott] once this comes to trial and he's under oath. You'd think these guys would have learned after the Aruba story not to make the same mistake twice," Sona said.

Later that April, it was revealed that the scope of the robocalls appeared to be limited to Guelph. Yves Côté, the commissioner of elections, issued his report on the scandal. He said that some confusing calls had been made, but the evidence didn't support claims that they were made to prevent people from voting. He said it was clear something had happened in Guelph, but that was part of another investigation. As such, Côté was not recommending any more charges.

According to the statistics compiled in Côté's report, there had been 379 complaints in Guelph about phone calls but no more than 34 in any other riding. In ridings where 15 or more complaints were filed, the number of people who said they didn't end up voting because of the call was less than one percent—a total of six out of 667 complaints.

"It's useful to note that the data gathered in the investigation does not lend support to the existence of a conspiracy or conspiracies to interfere with the voting process," Côté said.

Sona's trial began on June 2, 2014, in Guelph, Ontario. Much of the testimony at the trial mirrored exactly what had already been reported in the press. The initial testimony focused on the fact that two campaign workers said Sona approached them about automated phone calls that could not be traced back to anyone with the Burke campaign.

"I don't remember if I said I don't think it's a good idea or I thought it was a bad idea," John White said of his response to Sona's suggestion. White was also asked why he had downloaded that particular phone list from the CIMS database. He replied that he routinely downloaded those kinds of lists, so he couldn't really remember why he had downloaded this particular list.

White had, however, put Sona in touch with Matthew McBain, who worked for the national campaign in Ottawa. McBain testified that he didn't think Sona's idea was a good one.

"I had the impression he wanted to do an autodial phone call that would not be linked back to the Burke campaign. It didn't seem like the best use of time. They shouldn't be focussing on stunts but the regular things campaigns do," McBain said.

On June 4, Andrew Prescott, considered the star witness, took the stand. He testified that he had noticed a cellphone on Sona's desk, as well as packaging for a prepaid phone in a nearby garbage can. He told the court about election day, when Sona had emerged from a cubicle.

"I wasn't sure what he was doing, but he came out of his office at one point shaking, ecstatic and said in a low voice, 'It's working,'" Prescott testified.

Later, on election day, with the media reporting about the misleading calls, Morgan approached Prescott, gave him his log-on credentials for RackNine and asked him to cancel the call.

Prescott also recounted an anecdote from a party that had been held at the end of the campaign.

"Michael had a cigar in his hand…and said something along the lines of 'Thanks to Pierre.' And laughed," Prescott said.

Other witnesses included Docksteader, who testified that Sona told her he had used the name Pierre Poutine to set up the calls. Benjamin Hicks also testified that Sona told him the scheme was successful because it had "created chaos."

But the one person the court did not hear from was Ken Morgan. Morgan had moved to Kuwait in 2012 and had never spoken to Elections Canada investigators.

After the Crown finished with its witnesses, Boxall took the surprising step of not calling any witnesses. Sona did not testify in his own defence.

Sona was later found guilty. Judge Gary Hearn made it clear he felt there was more than one person involved:

Although the evidence indicates [Sona] did not likely act alone, he was party to the offence, and he was sentenced to nine months in jail plus one year on probation. In his ruling, Judge Hearn stated that Sona showed "a callous and blatant disregard for the people's right to vote" in this "ill-conceived and disturbing plan."

CHAPTER NINE

Omnibus Bills

ANOTHER EXAMPLE of how the Conservatives have continued to run roughshod over ability of Parliament to hold the government of the day to account is their ongoing abuse of the omnibus bill.

An omnibus bill is, essentially, a comprehensive bill that covers a diverse range and number of topics. Essentially it's several smaller pieces of legislation that have been crammed together into one bill. Sometimes the smaller pieces of legislation in the bill are related, but most often, especially as the Conservatives have been using them, little commonality exists among the various pieces of legislation. There is nothing inherently wrong with using an omnibus bill, especially if the changes within the bill are all related. However, the way the Harper government has used them poses a problem for Parliamentarians trying to hold the government to account. The bills tend to be massive in size, making it difficult for opposition Parliamentarians to give each proposed piece of legislation the attention it deserves. It is also difficult for Parliamentarians to vote on omnibus bills because they will likely support some parts of the bill but not others.

One of the best criticisms of the use of omnibus legislation actually comes ironically from Stephen

Harper himself. In 1994 the then Reform MP for Calgary Southwest was quoted as saying about omnibus bills:

> *First, there is a lack of relevancy of these issues. The omnibus bills we have before us attempt to amend several different existing laws. Second, in the interest of democracy I ask: How can members represent their constituents on these various areas when they are forced to vote in a block on such legislation and on such concerns? We can agree with some of the measures but oppose others. How do we express our views and the views of our constituents when the matters are so diverse? Dividing the bill into several components would allow members to represent views of their constituents on each of the different components in the bill.*

Funny the effect that power can have on a person's principles.

The Tories have typically used two different kinds of omnibus bills—crime bills and budget implementation acts. It is the latter that the Conservatives have been accused of abusing most often. Budget Implementation Acts are exactly what they sound like—acts that implement parts of a budget. But under the Conservatives, the budget implementation acts have become legislative monstrosities touching on scores of different pieces of legislation. An analysis by MacLean's showed that before the Conservatives came to power, the average length for budget implementation acts was 73.6 pages. Since the Conservatives came to power, those same bills now run an average of 308.9 pages.

The most recent, and in the opinion of many, the most egregious abuse of a Budget Implementation Act-turned-omnibus-bill came in the fall of 2013 when the government unveiled Bill C-4. But it wasn't the size of this particular bill—more than 300 pages—that garnered criticism. It wasn't the scope of the bill, which touched on a wide variety of topics, such as Supreme Court of Canada appointments, workplace safety, labour laws, veterans affairs, Employment Insurance, conflict-of-interest rules, solicitor-client privilege and immigration policy. It was its contents. This particular bill was criticized because it was a direct attack on the federal public service and its members' right to collective bargaining.

Among the changes to the act that the government brought forward in October 2013 was that, if passed, it would now be illegal for any bargaining unit to strike if it was deemed to provide an essential service. The problem with the proposed changes under Bill C-4 was that the government could unilaterally decide which professions in the public service constituted essential services. Such a declaration meant that members of a particular bargaining unit would not be allowed to strike. Previously any disagreement over what constituted an essential service could be referred to the Public Service Relations Board.

The exact wording of the bill stated: "The employer has the exclusive right to determine that service is essential and the number of positions required to provide that service."

The changes also denied unions the right to refer any dispute to arbitration unless more than 80 per cent of workers are deemed essential. So the government could simply declare up to 79 per cent of workers essential, thereby denying them the right to arbitration of any kind. The scope of the changes was wide. Of the

187,000 members of the Public Service Alliance of Canada (PSAC), 40,000 were considered essential at the time the bill was brought forward. Under Bill C-4, the government could increase those numbers dramatically.

The government insisted these changes were meant to save Canadians money. A government press release stated:

The proposed amendments will bring savings, streamline practices, and bring them in line with other jurisdictions. Our government will sit at a bargaining table on behalf of the taxpayer where the rules are fair and balanced.

What the bill constituted was more of an attack on the public service in line with the government's treatment of the federal work force over the previous two years. In that time the government had criticized federal workers for being overpaid and taking too many days off, saying that the average federal public service worker took 18 sick days per year. A series of statistics later released by Statistics Canada that contrasted absences in both the public and private sector showed that public sector servants actually took closer to 12 days off per year, compared to just over seven for the private sector. The study also found that, of the approximately five days difference between public and private sector workers, 80 percent of the five more absences in the public sector could be explained by the fact that the public service employed more older people and more women.

PSAC was highly critical of the proposed changes.

"This bill represents a far-reaching attack on public service workers and the unions that represent them," said PSAC president Robyn Benson. "The government is upsetting the balance of labour relations and is showing a callous disregard for due process, health and safety and the collective bargaining rights of every single public service employee."

Benson went on to say, "The collective bargaining rights and the protections of workers who face discrimination, who do dangerous work or who are treated unfairly will be undermined by the proposals in this bill."

Any hope of a thorough debate of the bill in the House of Commons was also quashed soon after the bill was unveiled. Introduced on a Tuesday in the House, the government announced two days later it would limit debate on second reading before the bill was sent off to hearings at committee. Debate would end after another two days.

The bill was sent to committee and passed third reading in the House of Commons in December, making its way into the Senate for approval. PSAC announced it would fight the changes in court. On March 27, the union filed its constitutional challenge to the bill. In its filing, the union argued that the bill violated federal workers freedom to strike and freedom of association guaranteed in the Canadian Charter of Rights and Freedoms.

The reaction on the part of unions to Bill C-4 was strong, but it didn't come close to the response of First Nations Canadians to provisions in another of the Harper government's omnibus Budget Implementation Acts. Bill C-45, introduced in late 2012, played a significant role in the Idle No More protests that rolled across Canada beginning in December 2012.

The sweeping act, which weighed in at approximately 450 pages, proposed changes to several different pieces of legislation, including the Fisheries Act, the Navigable Waters Protection Act and the Indian Act, as well as almost a dozen other pieces of legislation.

But it was the changes to the Indian Act that created significant opposition across Canada's First Nations population. The changes to the act made it easier for band leaders to lease out protected lands without having to gain community support. It effectively cut down on First Nations peoples' ability to protect their own lands by not allowing an opportunity for opposition groups to weigh in. Previously, the Indian Act required any changes to be passed by a majority of eligible voters. The specific changes in Bill C-45 allowed for land to be redesignated if a majority of attendees voted in favour at a meeting called for that purpose. Essentially, all that was now required was a meeting instead of a referendum.

First Nations were also concerned about changes to other acts. Under the Navigable Waters Protection Act, major pipeline and power line project advocates would no longer be required to prove their project wouldn't damage or destroy any navigable waterway that it crossed. Exempt were any waterways on a list prepared by the transportation minister. According to the CBC, Idle No More stated that the amendments removed protections for 99.9 per cent of lakes and rivers in Canada.

Changes to the Environmental Assessment Act were also criticized, as they reduced the number of projects that would require assessments.

Anger over the changes to these acts spread throughout the First Nations communities in Canada before erupting nationally in a series of protests and rallies. In concert with the protests, Theresa Spence, chief of the Attawapiskat First Nation, announced a hunger strike. During the course of her 43-day hunger strike, Spence camped out on an island in the Ottawa River and repeatedly called for meetings with Stephen Harper and the Governor General. No meeting was held.

The protests had no impact. The bill, unchanged, received Royal Assent on December 14, 2012.

The Harper government has also used omnibus bills to ram through crime legislation. In 2008, the Conservatives first introduced Bill C-2, otherwise known as the Tackling Violent Crime Act. The bill as proposed was meant to "protect Canadians from those who commit serious and violent crimes."

The bill featured a wide-ranging series of proposed changes to the Criminal Code of Canada. It created reverse onus bail provisions for individuals accused in serious gun crimes and other weapons-related offences. This meant that in order to be granted bail in these cases, the accused now had to prove why he should be granted bail when the Crown felt the accused should be kept in pre-trial custody. Previous to the change, it was up to the Crown to prove why an accused should be kept in custody until trial.

The bill also created new offences such as breaking and entering to steal a firearm and robbery to steal a firearm. It introduced mandatory minimum sentences for firearms offences, such as gun trafficking, requiring anywhere from three to five years for a first offence, five to seven for a second and eight for a third offence. The bill also raised the age of sexual consent from age 14 to 16 and created a three strikes law aimed at dangerous and high-risk offenders.

The legislation, though passed by Parliament, quickly ran into trouble in the courts. One judge in Ontario struck down a part of the bill that streamlined how repeat offenders could be deemed dangerous offenders. While in the past it was up to the Crown to prove that an individual should be categorized as a dangerous offender, the act now stated that anyone convicted of certain offences three times could be automatically designated a dangerous offender, and it was up to the defendant to prove otherwise.

Judges also began ignoring the mandatory minimum provisions outlined in the act for certain gun crimes. In two cases in Ontario, judges struck down the mandatory minimum sentences they were required to give the accused in each case.

The government also introduced Bill C-10 in 2012 as the Safe Streets and Communities Act. Also an omnibus bill, this particular piece of legislation introduced mandatory minimum sentences in cases of child exploitation and some major drug offences. One part of the bill was designed to allow Canada's security services enhanced powers for monitoring online communications, but the government chose to abandon it when an online petition garnered some 70,000 signatures.

The bill still ran into problems in its stripped-down form as critics said it would lead to overcrowding in prisons. Both Quebec and Ontario announced that they opposed the legislation and would not pay the costs of implementing it. Despite those protests, the bill received Royal Assent on March 13, 2012.

As shown, Stephen Harper's Conservatives like to use omnibus bills to ram unpalatable laws through the House of Commons. It is a tactic they will no doubt continue to use as long as they are in power.

CHAPTER TEN

Senate Expense Scandal

THE CANADIAN SENATE has, in modern times, not been held in the highest esteem across the country. Few Canadians would likely declare any interest in what the Red Chamber actually does on a day-to-day basis. Its business and debates seldom make the pages of any newspaper. Those Canadians who pay a little more attention to national affairs view it as a unelected house of patronage where former hockey players, singers and political party sycophants are rewarded with a plum appointment to the Senate for their loyalty to whichever party is presently in power. The job comes with a base salary of approximately $132,000 per year, which can be topped up by sitting on any of the Senate's committees. Senators could also, up until the most recent scandal, be reimbursed for a wide range of housing and travel expenses.

But the latest scandal not only saw the Senate make some changes to how it reimburses its members, it also gave the house of "sober second thought" an egregious reputation, this one as a corrupt institution of lies and shenanigans when a quartet of senators—three of them sitting as members of the Conservative Party—were accused of trying to claim ineligible expenses to the tune of hundreds of thousands of dollars.

The senators involved were Mike Duffy, Pamela Wallin, Patrick Brazeau and Mac Harb (a Liberal). Duffy, Wallin and Brazeau were appointed to the senate in 2009. Duffy and Wallin had both been nationally respected journalists in their careers. In fact, Duffy had worked on Parliament Hill as a broadcast journalist for CTV right up until he was appointed to the Senate. Brazeau's appointment had taken many on Parliament Hill by surprise, because he was only 34 years old at the time of his appointment. But Brazeau had helped the Conservatives in the last election before his appointment, when he had, as the national chief for the Congress of Aboriginal Peoples, endorsed Harper and the Conservatives. His appointment was seen as a reward for his support.

Mac Harb was appointed to the Senate in 2003 as a Liberal Senator. He was formerly an Ottawa city councillor and had served as a Liberal member of Parliament between 1988 and 2003.

Mike Duffy's residency had been an issue since he was first named to the Senate. All senators are required to keep a primary residence in the province or territory that they are supposed to represent. In Duffy's case, he had been appointed to represent Prince Edward Island, and he kept a home there, of sorts—a cottage near Cavendish, PEI. The media were especially skeptical of Duffy's appointment because he had purchased a home with his wife in Kanata, just outside Ottawa but was still claiming the cottage in Cavendish as his primary residence.

It wasn't just the issue of residency, and Duffy's residency specifically, that was making waves. At issue was the housing allowance to which most senators were entitled. That allowance permitted any senator whose primary residence was farther than 100 kilometres from Ottawa to claim up to $21,000 annually in living expenses. It was meant to compensate senators for the expenses they incurred as a result of having to work in two different places—their home province or territory and Ottawa. But reports began to emerge that some senators were submitting housing allowance expense claims despite the fact that they lived in or near Ottawa. As a result of the criticism, the Senate decided to look into the matter a little more closely. The investigation originally started with Brazeau's expenses and was then widened to include Duffy, Wallin and Harb.

In response to the ongoing argument over whether or not Duffy qualified as a resident of Prince Edward Island, one of the Senate committees asked for documentation to support declarations signed by senators that they lived in their home provinces. The Standing Committee on Internal Economy, Budgets and Administration asked for copies of senators' driver's licences and healthcare cards, as well as pages from their tax returns. They also requested signed letters indicating where each senator had voted in the last municipal, provincial and federal elections.

In February 2013, as the Senate was looking into housing claims, news reached the media that Mike Duffy had asked the health minister of PEI to speed up his application for a provincial healthcare card for that province. The news raised eyebrows—if Duffy was already a PEI resident, shouldn't he already have a PEI healthcare card? The minister replied that he saw no reason to fast track Duffy's application for the healthcare card.

But it wasn't just Duffy that the Senate was investigating. There were also rumours about the impropriety of expense claims made by Senators Pamela Wallin and Patrick Brazeau. Brazeau claimed a primary residence in Maniwaki, Québec, but also kept a home in Gatineau, a stone's throw from Ottawa. Wallin co-owned some properties in Wadena, Saskatchewan, had an address there that was a postal box and owned a plot of land in the hamlet of North Shore Fishing Lake. But she also had a home in downtown Toronto and had not lived in Saskatchewan for decades.

Meanwhile, Brazeau was making other news in court. On February 8, he appeared in court after being arrested and spending the previous night in jail in Gatineau. Police had been called to his home after someone called 911. Brazeau was charged with assault and sexual assault as a result of the incident. He was later released on $1000 bail under the conditions that he not possess any firearms and stay 150 metres away from the possible victim of the crime, who was not named publicly. The judge said that she expected him to live at his home in Maniwaki, even though he had another residence in Gatineau.

When asked about Brazeau's arrest, Stephen Harper replied that the situation was "extremely appalling. We all feel very let down."

"When Mr. Brazeau was appointed to the Senate, he was the national chief of one of the country's largest and most respected Aboriginal organizations. The events that we're speaking of here are very recent in nature. Obviously over a recent period, something has been going very wrong, and that is the reason for the situation that has developed," Harper said.

The Senate announced that, in light of the arrest, it planned to force Brazeau to take a leave. He would still receive his base salary of $132,000, but he would need Senate approval for any other expenses. He was also removed from the Conservative caucus.

On February 11, the leaders of the two parties in the Senate, Conservative Senator Marjory LeBreton and Liberal Senator James Cowan, issued a joint letter to the internal economy committee that was investigating the senators' housing claims. In the letter, the two asked the committee to do the following: "We request that you proceed to interview each senator who has claimed a secondary residence allowance to confirm the legitimacy of such claims. Should any senator be unable to convince you that the claim is valid, that senator should be required to repay immediately all monies so paid with interest."

The two also stipulated what they expected if any discrepancies were found: "We believe it is vital for the reputation of the Senate and those senators who are in full compliance with our rules and regulations that this determination be made as soon as possible and that the result be made public," the letter said.

At the same time, the committee confirmed that it had referred claims by Duffy, Brazeau and Harb to the auditing firm Deloitte. It also said it was seeking special legal advice on the issue of Duffy's residency.

Claiming a housing allowance wasn't a rare occurrence—it was revealed that since 2011, only seven senators had not claimed some sort of allowance. Of those that did, 40 had made claims for hotel rooms when they were in Ottawa on Senate business.

Duffy decided he needed to try to get out in front of the audit that was taking place. On February 22, he announced that he would pay back his housing allowance claims, admitting that he shouldn't have received money for them. He blamed the mistakes on paperwork, which he said he found confusing.

"The Senate rules on housing allowances aren't clear, and the forms are confusing. I filled out the Senate forms in good faith and believed I was in compliance with the rules. Now it turns out I may have been mistaken," he said.

Since 2010, he had claimed $33,000 in living allowances.

"Rather than let this issue drag on, my wife and I have decided that the allowance associated with my house in Ottawa will be repaid," Duffy said.

The announcement was met with skepticism and criticism from the Opposition.

"How could it be that you can fill out forms to collect money you're not entitled to and then you have to get caught, you have to get hounded to pay it back and then you can just shrug and say, 'Catch me the next time.' That's not good enough," said NDP ethics critic Charlie Angus.

On February 28, it was reported that beyond Wallin, Duffy, Brazeau and Harb, no other questionable housing allowance claims had been uncovered. Wallin was apparently already repaying some of the claims she'd had made, which were believed to total approximately $321,000. However, questions still persisted about whether or not Duffy and Wallin even qualified as Senators, but Harper made it clear that there was no confusion on the issue in his mind, saying both met the residency requirement.

"That is the basis on which they are appointed to the Senate, and those requirements have been clear for 150 years," Harper said.

By April 18, it was not yet known for certain if Duffy had kept his promise to repay the money he owed. When asked, Marjory LeBreton, the leader of the government in the Senate, said she had not received any formal report that Duffy had paid anything back. When confronted about it by the press, Duffy replied, "I'm a man of my word."

Liberal Senator Roméo Dallaire said he thought the brewing scandal was giving the Senate a poor reputation across Canada.

"The whole scenario has been a terrible misfortune for the Senate. One, people don't know what we do, and two, the only thing they hear is all this crap. They better sort it out," said Dallaire.

On April 19, word came that Duffy had, in fact, repaid his housing allowance claims. The total, however, was much larger than many had been led to believe. He had repaid exactly $90,172.24, almost triple the $33,000 in claims he had made since 2010.

It took almost another month, but the Senate finally received and then released the audit from Deloitte on May 9. The audit revealed that Duffy had only spent 30 percent of his time at his cottage in PEI, casting his claim of it being his primary residence in doubt. For Harb, only 21 percent of his time had been spent at the home he claimed as his primary residence, while Brazeau had spent only 10 percent of his time at the home in Maniwaki he claimed was his primary residence.

The public was instantly furious, but Harper said there were no real problems.

"The auditor has concluded that the rules in place were not clear; however, the Senate itself has decided it expects better judgment from the Senators," he said.

But there were signs that Duffy might have actually been tipped off about the audit findings and some of the irregularities in his claims. A letter from Duffy to Senator David Tkachuk, the Conservative chairman of the internal economy committee, stated that he was aware auditors had found he had collected more than $1000 as a daily living allowance while he was actually on a 12-day vacation in Florida.

"Following our informal conversation Tuesday evening, I went through my files for January 2012. I discovered that through a clerical error, per diems were inadvertently charged for several days when I was not in the National Capital Region," the letter said. The letter had been sent on April 16, the same day Tkachuk was briefed by auditors on its findings. Duffy blamed the claim on a temporary staffer.

"The claim was clearly not appropriate and I will reimburse the Senate without hesitation," Duffy wrote in the letter.

But Duffy wasn't alone in having been found to have submitted questionable claims. As a result of the audit, Mac Harb was asked to repay $51,500, and Patrick Brazeau was asked to repay approximately $49,000.

Any senator discovered to have made irregular housing claims would simply be asked to repay the amount owing, LeBreton had said, and the matter would be considered closed. That meant the three wouldn't face charges of fraud.

But the internal economy committee decided it should have a closer look at the expenses for Harb and Brazeau. The committee decided to look at a few additional years of expense claims. For Harb, they went back another seven years, and for Brazeau, another two. Harb replied that he was quitting the Liberal caucus to fight the matter in court.

Despite LeBreton's assertion that the matter would be considered closed for any senator who repaid the amount owing, the RCMP decided to take a look anyway. James Cowan had already stated publicly that they should investigate, and on May 12, the RCMP said they would look at Senate expense claims for housing and travel expenses for Brazeau, Duffy and Harb. They wouldn't say whether or not they were starting a criminal investigation, only that the National Division to Focus on Sensitive and International Investigations would be taking a look.

But Cowan also noted some strange discrepancies in the language used in the committee's report into the matter. While it had stated with respect to Harb and Brazeau that the rules on residency were "amply clear," that same statement was nowhere to be found in the discussion of Duffy's housing claims.

"Why? I think that's a very important question," Cowan said.

In the wake of the audit and their own findings, the committee proposed 11 rule changes, including eliminating almost all international travel claims and limiting the number of domestic flights that could be claimed.

But the issue was not settled yet. The scandal reached new heights on May 15, when CTV revealed that Nigel Wright, the chief of staff for Prime Minister Stephen Harper, had given Duffy the $90,000 he needed to repay his expenses.

When asked, senior government officials said that Harper himself didn't know about the payment until it was revealed publicly. It also came to light that Duffy had stopped working with the auditors after he had used Wright's money to pay back his claims.

"What we're dealing with here is a very unusual set of facts. There will be a lot of people drawing their own independent conclusions, and this could be an absolute morass of unanswered issues and questions," said Liberal Ralph Goodale in reaction to the news.

The Prime Minister's Office stated that Wright had loaned Duffy the money because "Duffy was unable to make a timely payment."

"Mr. Wright therefore wrote a cheque from his personal account for the full amount owing so that Mr. Duffy could repay the outstanding amount," said Andrew MacDougall, a spokesperson for Stephen Harper. He added there was no expectation that Duffy would have to pay back the money.

Ethics commissioner Mary Dawson announced she would be reviewing the case "and is following up with Mr. Wright."

The speculation was that the payment, besides seeming improper, could be construed as a bribe. There were several pieces of legislation that made giving money to a sitting Parliamentarian an offence—the Senate Conflict of Interest Code stated that no senator or family member was allowed to receive a gift except for "compensation authorized by law." Similar provisions exist in the Parliament of Canada Act and the Criminal Code of Canada. Violations could include prison sentences ranging from one to five years.

The following day, in the wake of the announcement, as public fury over the news was mounting, Duffy announced that he was leaving the Conservative caucus to sit as an Independent. But there were reports that he was pressured to do so. Sources told the media that a large majority of the Senators had signed a petition calling for Duffy to be booted from caucus, and they were ready to present the petition to Duffy at their next meeting.

"Given that my presence within the Conservative caucus only contributes to that distraction, I have decided to step outside of the caucus and sit as an Independent senator pending resolution of these questions," Duffy announced.

The prime minister was said to still have confidence in his chief of staff and would not be firing him, but more news was still coming out about Duffy. Reports surfaced that he had actually billed the Senate for travel expenses while campaigning in the 2011 election. But such expenses, considered partisan in nature, should only be reimbursed by the Conservative Party, not the Senate.

More details also emerged about the arrangement that saw Wright give Duffy the money he needed. At first, the sole expectation on Duffy for receiving the money was to pay it back as quickly as possible. It was revealed that Wright wrote the cheque to Duffy's lawyer in trust. Duffy had also apparently taken out a loan to cover the cost of repayment of his housing and travel claims and had gotten the loan without Wright's involvement. But there appeared to be conditions on Duffy's agreement to pay back the money. It was revealed that in return for repaying the money, the final report on expenses would go easy on Duffy. And Duffy himself was also supposed to keep quiet about the housing claims.

It was also revealed that although Brazeau and Harb had met with auditors during their investigation, Duffy had, through his lawyer, sent the auditors a letter the day after he repaid the money, saying his participation in the audit was "no longer needed." No further documentation was provided to the auditors on Duffy's behalf. Duffy had offered to meet with the auditors on April 20, but the idea was rejected because it would further delay the audit report.

There was more bad news the following day. Pamela Wallin's expenses were still being audited, but in advance of a report on her expenses, she announced that she was quitting the Conservative caucus. The audit was specifically looking at her claims for more than $300,000 in travel expenses.

"I have been involved in the external audit process since December 2012, and I have been cooperating fully and willingly with the auditors," Wallin said.

"I have met with the auditors, answered all questions and provided all requested documentation."

She also said she thought the process would be finished by now.

"I had anticipated that the audit process would be complete by now, but given that it continues, I have decided to recuse myself from the Conservative caucus, and I will have no further comment until the audit process is complete," Wallin said.

But Wallin wasn't the only one in the news. The Senate announced that it was sending Duffy's expenses back to the internal economy committee for further review.

"In light of [Thursday's] media reports regarding Senator Duffy's expense claims, senators will be asking that the report concerning Senator Duffy be referred back to committee for further examination taking into account this new information," said a spokesperson for Marjory LeBreton.

Harper's trust and confidence in his chief of staff didn't last long. On May 19, Nigel Wright resigned from his position.

Conservatives hoping for some sign of contrition or humility from their leader as a result of the ongoing scandal in the Senate were disappointed. Harper addressed his Conservative caucus on May 21 but reportedly did not issue any kind of apology or show any sign of remorse over what had taken place. Many Conservatives, though they wouldn't give their names, later told the media that they were not impressed.

"Honest backbenchers didn't start this mess—it started at the centre. There needs to be an apology to caucus and the public," said one MP. "One rule-breaker is bad, but three, plus the chief of staff, is a systemic problem. The real problem is, we crossed the moral red line a long time ago."

The Liberals were calling on the Conservatives to make public the entire review of Duffy's expenses. James Cowan called on the internal economy committee to hold their hearings on Duffy's expenses in public.

"Let's open the process up, let's give everybody an opportunity to be heard and we can see who says what when, then we'll know," Cowan said.

Duffy also issued a statement in response to the new revelations.

"Canadians deserve to know all of the facts. I am confident that when they do, they will conclude as Deloitte has already concluded, that my actions regarding expenses do not merit criticism," Duffy said.

The media, meanwhile, had gotten their hands on a draft copy of the internal economy committee's first report into the three senators' expenses. They found that some changes had been made to the section that discussed Duffy's expenses. Specifically, they found that a paragraph about Duffy's refusal to meet with the auditors at Deloitte had been deleted. Another section saying that the language regarding what constitutes a primary residence was "unambiguous" had also been dropped from the report. As well, it was discovered that the Liberals on the committee had voted against the final report before it had been released.

When asked about whether or not the senators had agreed to go easy on Duffy in exchange for him paying back the $90,000 he owed, Marjory LeBreton replied, "That is an allegation that I have absolutely no proof of."

Stephen Harper was still telling anyone who asked that he knew nothing of the payment from Wright to Duffy.

"Look, I think my belief here was reasonable...that when it was said that Mr. Duffy had repaid his expenses, that indeed he—and not someone else—had repaid his expenses. I know Mr. Wright assisted him or did this for him, because he wanted to see the taxpayers reimbursed. That's the right motive, but nevertheless it was obviously not correct for that decision to be made and executed without my knowledge, or without public transparency," Harper said.

The news began to hit the Conservatives hard in public opinion polls. A new poll for the *National Post* of 1779 Canadians showed that the Liberals would likely secure a majority government if an election were held immediately. They had the support of 44 percent of those polled, compared to 27 percent for the Conservatives and 20 percent for the NDP.

Duffy was adamant he was not going to resign, even as the news for him grew increasingly worse. He even called for a public inquiry into his expenses.

"We need a full and open inquiry so that it all gets aired. I think Canadians have a right to know all the facts and I'm quite prepared, in the right place and time, to give them the whole story," Duffy said to reporters.

The RCMP were now asking for documents regarding the Senate's travel and expense policies. The Conservatives in the Senate were still on the defensive about allegations that the committee had altered its report to "go easy" on Mike Duffy. The chair of the committee, David Tkachuk, said that the Prime Minister's Office had contacted him while he was overseeing the audit of Duffy's expenses but claimed that no one told him to do anything. He said they only asked about the audit process and when the final report about Duffy would be made public.

"They never asked me to do anything wrong. I was never directed to do anything," Tkachuk said.

Public opinion of the Senate was also falling. A new poll showed that only one person in 10 said they would keep the Senate in its current form. Of those surveyed, 51 percent said they had a poor opinion of the Senate. And 70 percent of those polled said they thought Duffy and Wallin should resign.

On May 28, the internal economy committee voted unanimously to refer Duffy's expense reports to the RCMP. The committee heard that he had claimed per diems on 49 days between April 2011 and March 2012, when records showed he might not even have been in Ottawa. He had received payment for 25 of those days. The committee added that what had happened with respect to Duffy claiming expenses when he was on vacation in Florida "was not an isolated incident." The committee also voted to hold all hearings about Duffy's claims in public.

The Senate voted to tighten its spending rules. It scrapped the honour system that had governed all senators in the past when making expense claims. All claims would now need to be accompanied by proper receipts to qualify for reimbursement.

During Question Period, the opposition continued to demand more answers from the Conservatives.

"We're asking very simple, straightforward questions and the prime minister's not answering them. Mike Duffy wrote in an email that after being paid $90,000, he 'stayed silent on the orders of the Prime Minister's Office.' Who told Mike Duffy to remain silent?" Thomas Mulcair, leader of the NDP, asked.

Harper replied, "The facts here are very straightforward. This is a matter between Mr. Wright and Mr. Duffy. It is the subject of an examination by the ethics commissioners in both Houses of Parliament."

It also appeared that the base salary for Senators was not good enough for Mike Duffy. On May 30, the CBC revealed that Duffy had been trying to get himself either named to cabinet or given some other perks when he was appointed to the Senate. Emails from July 2009, just six months after he was appointed, showed that he was talking with the Conservatives about an expanded position with additional compensation, such as being named a minister without portfolio so that he could get a car and staff. Although senators can be named to cabinet, it is highly unusual because senators are appointed rather than elected.

The press revealed the next day that Duffy had actually approached Harper at a fundraiser back in February 2013 to discuss his expense claims. A spokesperson for the prime minister said that Harper had only told Duffy that any inappropriate expenses should be repaid.

Duffy told reporters that he believed he would inevitably be vindicated.

"When that work is done, I think that Canadians will agree, as the independent auditors at Deloitte found, that criticism of my expenses is, frankly, largely without merit," he said to reporters in PEI.

But the news was getting increasingly worse for all the senators embroiled in the scandal. On June 12, the internal economy committee released its new findings of Mac Harb's expenses. He was now on the hook for $230,000 in living expenses, more than four times what he had originally said he owed. The review of seven years of expenses showed that he was not spending enough time at his primary residence in Westmeath, Ontario. Before living in Westmeath, Harb had been living in Cobden. The audit found that he had spent only 20 percent of his time at either residence when he was living in either location. The Senate officially issued letters calling for Harb and Brazeau to pay back their amounts owing. The Senate could, the public learned, garnish their wages if they didn't start making payments. Wallin had already paid back some of her expenses; those payments were said to be $38,000, but no one yet knew just how much she would have to repay in total.

The RCMP were widening the scope of their investigation. On June 13, they announced that they were now launching a formal investigation into Nigel Wright's conduct, saying that a full investigation was needed "to determine whether a criminal act has taken place." A week later, a release of documents showed that they were also investigating Harb. They had obtained property documents for the home he had owned in Cobden. The force was also combing through the tax returns of 11 Conservative candidates Duffy had campaigned for in the last election. The documents showed that the RCMP were pursuing charges of breach of trust against Duffy, but none had yet been laid.

A new round of court documents from the RCMP on July 6 added more intrigue to the scandal. The documents confirmed that the RCMP were pursuing charges of fraud in addition to the breach of trust charges. The documents showed that a small inner circle of individuals in the Prime Minister's Office knew about Wright's payment to Duffy. It was also confirmed that there had been two conditions attached to the loan—to pay off the expenses owing immediately and to stop talking to the media. The document outright stated that Duffy "has demonstrated a pattern of filing fraudulent expense claims."

It was also alleged that the Conservatives were at first planning to pay off Duffy's debt from the Conservative Fund of Canada. The fund, which the media reported could at times reach balances of close to $1 million, holds money for the Conservatives. A great deal of the money—the CBC estimated half of the total—comes from donations. And those donors are usually taxpayers. But when the Conservatives learned the true amount that Duffy would have to repay, they vetoed the idea of using the fund to pay off his expenses.

The Canadian Taxpayers Federation decided to make some hay out of the whole Duffy affair. The group, which purports to represent Canadian taxpayers, staged an event on July 18 in which it unveiled its new mascot, a 10-metre-tall, inflatable version of Mike Duffy, complete with a briefcase of cash.

"Two thousand, one hundred and fifty cubic feet of hot air, with a grossly inflated sense of his own self-importance and a giant bag of taxpayers' money," explained spokesperson Gregory Thomas.

On August 13, Deloitte came back with its audit of Pamela Wallin's expenses. The news was not good. It was determined that of the $532,508 she had claimed in expenses, $390,192 was appropriate. That meant that, when the $38,000 she had already repaid was factored in, she still owed the Senate another $120,000. Deloitte even made the unusual recommendation that she be prohibited from flying unless the Senate granted her permission. Part of the reason was the fact that she flew frequently and often included overnight stopovers in Toronto on her flights from Saskatchewan to Ottawa, which could easily be accomplished in a day with time leftover. In fact, she had claimed $29,432 in flights between 2010 and 2012. She had a home in Toronto, where she spent 35 percent of her time, compared to the 27 percent of her time spent in Saskatchewan.

The audit also found that Wallin had altered her Outlook calendar while the audit was taking place. The changes included adding several items called "Senate business" that were not in the original copy of the Outlook calendar the auditors had received. Other events were made to look less partisan than they had originally appeared. One event entitled "Saskatoon Event (4-riding fundraiser)" was edited to say only "Saskatoon Event." Wallin said the changes were the result of a formatting process aimed at co-operating with the audit.

"At no time did I attempt to mislead Deloitte in any way. We knew that Deloitte had a copy of the original calendars available to them at all times," Wallin said.

There were also indications that she had claimed travel expenses to attend events for the Conservative Party and for the Ontario PC Party, as well as corporate functions for Porter Airlines, where she had a seat on the board. Wallin also claimed expenses for attending the 2011 Juno Awards and for participating in a federal election night discussion panel, for which she had represented the federal party.

The news was enough for the auditor general. On August 15, Michael Ferguson announced that he would conduct an audit of the expenses of every member of the Senate. The report was expected in 18 months.

The first few months of that audit were difficult for Ferguson when it came to finding Senators in Ottawa. On August 19, Stephen Harper announced that he would talk to the Governor General about proroguing Parliament. Harper said that he was doing so because the Conservatives had accomplished all of their objectives for the current sitting of Parliament and a reset was needed with a new Speech from the Throne. The opposition, however, pointed to Harper's previous prorogations as proof that he was simply trying to get away from the growing scandal.

"He's running away from accountability," said NDP deputy leader Megan Leslie.

"It's a pattern with him, where he wants to avoid those uncomfortable questions, then he just hits the prorogue button.

On August 26, Mac Harb announced his resignation from the Senate. He had just paid back the $231,000 he owed.

"The Senate committee treated me very unfairly, and I wanted to make the point that every Canadian, even senators, should be entitled to due process. I always followed Senate rules on expenses, and filed my expense claims in a timely and transparent manner. At no time did anyone suggest my claims were invalid or questionable. And from what I could tell, most senators made similar claims," Harb said.

But the break didn't offer Harper much relief from the Senate scandal. On September 26, the RCMP revealed that they were interviewing other senators about Wallin's travel expenses. Then, on October 8, another RCMP document filed in court showed that Duffy had allegedly secured payment of $65,000 from the Senate for an individual who claimed he had done "no tangible work." The man was Gerald Donohue, a friend of Duffy's and a TV technician by training. While Duffy had stated that Donohue's duties were to include speechwriting, working on Duffy's website, helping with a heritage project and assisting with a project on the aging population, Donohue himself told the RCMP that all he really did was watch the news and tell Duffy what he had seen. All the payments were made by cheque to Donohue's media company. Donohue also said that he never sent any of the money back to Duffy, and he didn't receive any of the money personally because he was accepting disability payments.

On October 17, the Senate began the process of suspending Brazeau, Duffy and Wallin from the Senate. The move would strip them of their salaries, benefits and resources for the remainder of the Parliamentary session, which could last as long as two years.

"It's not a question of money, it's a question of gross misconduct," said Senate leader Claude Carignan. "It's very severe sanctions, but I think it's appropriate in this case."

Despite their outrage, some in the Senate were hesitant about the move owing to the fact that none of the three senators had been formally charged as a result of their disputed expense claims. Brazeau still faced criminal charges, but those had nothing to do with his Senate expenses.

"This is an extraordinary measure brought in at a time with the government who are seeking public favour because they're down in the polls—it's the popular thing to do. Under Senate rules, the upper chamber can take whatever actions it needs to protect itself, even if it means withdrawing the parliamentary privileges of its members," said Liberal senator George Baker.

All three decided to fight the move. On October 23, Duffy stood in the Red Chamber to protest the unpaid suspension. He told the Senate that the prime minister had ordered him to pay the money back. He said he was told that if he didn't pay the money back, the Conservatives in the Senate would issue a press release saying he was "unqualified" to sit as a senator. He was also told that the report from the internal economy committee would go easy on him.

The prime minister, Duffy said, "wasn't interested in explanations or the truth. It's not about what you did. It's about the perception of what you did that has been created by the media."

Wallin said that the Senate had no business trying to suspend her or her two other colleagues when they had not yet been found guilty of any crime.

She said there was a "palpable apprehension of bias in what I contend is a purely politically motivated set of charges in a chamber that has not demonstrated it is prepared to rise above party politics…why is the Senate acting as accuser, judge, jury and executioner before I've had that day in court?" she asked.

The following day, LeBreton dismissed what Duffy had said the Conservatives would do to him.

"The story that Senator Duffy spun in this place is not based in facts and it certainly leaves open to question what he was talking about and what he was thinking. There's no joy in having this whole situation before us," said LeBreton.

She said on May 16 that she had called Duffy to tell him he had two choices—he could leave caucus of his own accord or she would kick him out.

Duffy kept talking. On October 28, he revealed that there were actually two sums that were paid. While Wright had helped him pay the $90,000, the Conservative Party had covered his legal expenses, which totalled $13,560. Nigel Wright had apparently told Conservative lawyer Arthur Hamilton to ensure those bills were paid.

"He paid my lawyer's legal fees. That's right, the PMO had the Conservative Party's lawyer, Arthur Hamilton, pay for my lawyer," Duffy said.

The party confirmed what Duffy said, which led to more questions in the House of Commons.

"If those expenses were 'clearly inappropriate,' why did the prime minister, whose own office controlled that fund, ask the Conservative Party lawyer to pay Mike Duffy's expenses? Why ask to help cover something up that he now claims was 'clearly inappropriate?'" Mulcair asked Harper in Question Period.

Patrick Brazeau gave it one last try on November 4, trying to prevent his colleagues from voting him, Duffy and Wallin out.

In a letter to the Senate, Brazeau wrote:

I recommend you have a lawyer examine all claims you submit before you submit them. You may currently believe you are being compliant with [House of Commons] or Senate policy. The rules may change without your knowledge and you may find yourself kicked out of your caucus, being suspended without pay and being scapegoated in the media.

But the letter didn't work. On November 5, the Senate voted to suspend all three. The only change to their suspensions was that they could keep their medical and dental benefits, as well as their life insurance. They would also still qualify for their pensions. The specific votes to suspend each senator were 52–27 with 12 abstentions for Pamela Wallin; 52–28 with 11 abstentions for Mike Duffy; and 50–29 for with 13 abstentions for Patrick Brazeau.

Within two weeks, more RCMP documents surfaced with more assertions about the senators. The new documents showed that the RCMP believed Wright broke the law when he gave Duffy the $90,000. They also confirmed that a plan was in place to lighten the language in the report about Duffy's expenses. The document also made a statement that cast some doubt on what the prime minister had known. One email from Wright said that, "The PM knows, in broad terms only, that I personally assisted Duffy when I was getting him to agree to the expenses."

Harper continued to stick to his story.

"He didn't know. Period," said communications director Jason MacDonald.

In February 2014, the RCMP finally laid charges against one of the three when Patrick Brazeau was charged with breach of trust and fraud. There were also rumours that he was being investigated for tax evasion.

Three months later, Brazeau was back in court again, but not as a result of his Senate expenses. He'd been arrested again at his home in Gatineau and this time charged with two counts of simple assault, one count of cocaine possession, one count of threatening another person with death or injury and one count of breaching his release conditions from his arrest the previous year. Police had been called regarding a domestic assault complaint and found a man and woman engaged in a fight on the balcony of Brazeau's Gatineau home. A 50-year-old friend of the victim at the home had been threatened. When police searched Brazeau, they alleged that they found cocaine.

It was another sad chapter in Brazeau's fall from grace. After his expulsion from the Senate, he had tried working as a columnist for a magazine but was fired after writing one-and-a-half columns. He then accepted a job as a manager at a strip club.

On April 15, the RCMP announced that Nigel Wright would not face any charges.

"My intention was to secure the repayment of taxpayer funds. I believed that my actions were always in the public interest and lawful. The outcome of the RCMP's detailed and thorough investigation has now upheld my position," Wright said in a statement.

In June 2014, the RCMP revealed that when Duffy was in PEI, he had actually spent a lot of time staying at hotels in Charlottetown instead of at his cottage, at times charging the Senate more than $1000 a month for hotels for himself and his wife. Duffy said he often stayed there in the winter months because he had a heart condition. The RCMP also stated that between 2009 and 2011, Duffy had spent only about seven percent of the winter months—35 of 481 days—at his cabin. Records showed that he was at a hotel on nights he said he was at his cabin.

In July 2014, a woman living in Peru came forward claiming that Mike Duffy was her father. According to *Maclean's* magazine, Karen Duffy had tried to reach out to Duffy several times before she finally filed a lawsuit in Peruvian court. According to the magazine, the mother was a convicted drug smuggler who had served time in prison in Kingston.

Duffy replied in a statement: "The *Maclean's* story contains untrue allegations, made by a convicted narcotics smuggler, and which go back more than 30 years. I will respond to any legal process from Peru in an appropriate manner. I will have no further comment."

That same week, the RCMP held a press conference in which they revealed they had laid 31 charges against

Duffy in relation to the Senate spending scandal. In detail, those charges were as follows:

- With respect to claims in relation to residency, Duffy faces one count each of fraud over $5000 and breach of trust. The total amount of the alleged fraud counts is $90,000.

- With respect to expense claims unrelated to senate business, Duffy faces five counts of fraud under $5000, four counts of fraud over $5000 and nine counts of breach of trust. The total amount of the alleged fraud counts exceeds $50,000.

- With respect to consulting contracts, Duffy faces two counts of fraud over $5000, two counts of fraud under $5000 and four counts of breach of trust. The amount of the alleged fraud counts exceeds $60,000.

- The remaining counts, with respect to taking $90,000 from Nigel Wright, are one count each of bribery of a judicial officer, fraud on the government and breach of trust.

Among the new allegations revealed in documents related to the charges were that Duffy charged the Senate for travel to funerals and gave money to three people for what the RCMP called "illegitimate expenses." According to the *Ottawa Citizen*, one of those was a woman who did makeup work for a photo shoot, and a second was an individual who was working in the PMO at the time of this writing, but was not working in that capacity when the RCMP said the illegitimate expenses occurred. A third individual, according to the *Citizen*, was believed to be a personal trainer.

The charges have not yet been proven in court.

Duffy made the following statement in response to the charges: "This is a matter that's before the courts, and it would be inappropriate for me to comment at this time. I'm looking forward to appearing in court under oath and telling my story so Canadians will know the truth."

There was early speculation that Duffy might try to call Stephen Harper to testify in the upcoming trial. Pundits were unsure if the prime minister might try to avoid doing so by invoking his parliamentary privilege.

On July 23, it was revealed that Duffy had contacted Karen Duffy, the woman alleging Duffy was her father, and that the two had spoken during a two-hour Facetime conversation that was described by the CBC as "warm."

Duffy's trial will begin in April 2015. It is scheduled to last 41 days.

Conclusion

DURING MY YEARS as a reporter with the St. Albert Gazette, I was fortunate to form good professional relationships with many elected officials, including St. Albert's present member of Parliament, Brent Rathgeber. Brent's case is something of a scandal in and of itself. For those who might not be familiar with Brent, he was a dutiful Conservative backbencher until the summer of 2013, when he quit the Conservative caucus. The issue that prompted Brent's exit was the treatment that a bill of his received from the Prime Minister's Office. The bill, called the CBC and Public Service Disclosure and Transparency Act, would have made public the salaries of civil servants earning more than $188,000 per year. The PMO decided, without consulting Brent, to increase the salary threshold to $400,000, meaning that the salaries of deputy ministers would be protected. As a result, Brent made the striking decision to quit the caucus, making national headlines in the process and generating a significant amount of sympathy and support for his actions.

"Legislators like me have to take a stand," Brent said at the time. "We have to take a stand that we are not going to read these talking points written by staffers, that we're not going to vote like trained seals."

More telling still was the reaction of the man Brent replaced. Before Brent won the Conservative nomination in St. Albert, the city was represented by John Williams, who was first elected as a member of the Reform Party, then the Canadian Alliance, then the Conservative Party. It was John who chaired the public accounts committee when the Auditor General first unveiled the scope and breadth of what became the sponsorship scandal. When I called John to ask him for his thoughts on Brent's decision to quit the Conservative caucus, John praised Brent's decision, saying, "The Prime Minister must respect the opinions of his backbench..." Brent has since written his own book, *Irresponsible Government: The Decline of Parliamentary Democracy in Canada* and graciously wrote the Foreword for this book.

I found Brent's decision and John's support of it a striking indictment of Prime Minister Stephen Harper and the Conservative Party. Consider again, as alluded to earlier in this book, that the Conservatives made bold promises of accountability and transparency when they took over from the Liberals in the 2006 election. Brent was trying to further that promise, yet the prime minister decided that there is a limit to what Canadians need to know about the salaries of the nation's civil servants. Here were two men who were party supporters—John had supported his party in all of its different forms for the better part of two decades—and both were openly stating that Stephen Harper was wrong. Considering the strict discipline most political parties enforce, Brent's decision was reflective of the general discontent of people with the Harper Conservatives. That Brent quit the party in the heyday of the Senate spending scandal further added to the growing public frustration and discontent with the Harper government.

As of the writing of this book, the Conservatives appear to be in trouble nationally. As of the beginning of October 2014, three polling firms—Angus Reid Global,

Abacus Data and EKOS Research—all showed the Liberals with between 36 and 38 percent public support, compared to 24.9 to 30 percent for the Conservatives and the NDP around 22 and 23 percent. If an election were held today, the Conservatives would once again be relegated to the opposition benches, and Stephen Harper, most likely, would be out of a job. That being said, the most recent polls were taken only two weeks after the RCMP announced it was laying charges against Mike Duffy in the Senate spending scandal. It will be interesting to see how the numbers play out when that announcement is not so fresh in the public consciousness. One must keep in mind that the RCMP have yet to announce any charges against suspended senator Pamela Wallin. Considering the findings of the Deloitte auditors who looked at Wallin's spending, charges seem likely.

The Senate scandal as a whole may end up sinking Stephen Harper. Although no date has yet been sent in Mike Duffy's case, a trial date sometime before the fall of 2015 is possible. And that could definitely foul the Conservatives' election plan because the next federal election is scheduled to take place in the fall of 2015. Duffy's trial could be particularly damaging for Harper if he is subpoenaed to testify, a possibility that has been discussed at great length in the media. If Harper is subpoenaed to testify in court, under oath, about Duffy and the deal that Nigel Wright concluded with Duffy, three outcomes are possible: Harper will maintain that he knew nothing of the deal; Harper will say he knew of the deal; or Harper will invoke his parliamentary privilege to avoid testifying. None of these outcomes will benefit the Conservatives. It stands to reason that the optics would

CONCLUSION

be poor. The prime minister testifying in the case of an allegedly corrupt senator, even if he maintains, as he has all along, he knew nothing of the Duffy-Wright deal, would not benefit the Conservatives in the next election. Admitting he did know of the deal would be disastrous, considering Harper has always maintained he knew nothing. Invoking parliamentary privilege would just look like the prime minister is avoiding testifying, which might hurt the Conservatives even further.

It is difficult to predict what will happen in the fall of 2015, when Canadians head to the polls in the next federal election. When one looks at the broad litany of scandal that has taken place while the Conservatives have been in power, and couple that with the recent polling numbers that show the Liberals well ahead of the Conservatives, it would be easy to start predicting the Conservatives' demise. To discount them so early, however, would be a mistake. I was one of many who predicted another Conservative minority government in 2011 and was shocked when Canadians gave them a majority instead. Polling numbers have proven somewhat unreliable in the last four to five years. The outcomes in recent provincial elections in Alberta, Ontario and BC surprised many, as the polling numbers seemed to indicate the result should have been different in each case than what actually transpired. Politicians are always fond of saying that the only poll that matters is election day—a saying that has never been more true than in recent years.

One must also take into account the strength of the Conservatives' fundraising arm as the party routinely outperforms the opposition in total fundraising. In just the second quarter of 2014, the Conservatives raised

$4.7 million, compared to $2.8 million for the Liberals and $1.5 million for the NDP. Money is the lifeblood of any campaign, and the more one party can raise, the bigger an advantage it has over its competition.

One also can't discount the dogged fervour with which a party's stalwarts support it, and that goes for the Conservatives as well. Some people support their party unequivocally, regardless of scandal or poor performance. I remember the day after Brent Rathgeber announced his resignation from the Conservative caucus, the media descended on his downtown St. Albert office for a scrum. One of his supporters managed to sneak into the crowd of journalists all fighting to get close to Brent and started to express his dissatisfaction with Brent's actions. Because he wasn't a journalist, the individual was shouted down by most of the reporters before he could finish what he was saying, but the statement he was trying to make was pretty clear—he put his faith in the party first. How the party had treated Brent was of little or no concern.

That one man seemed to embody the Conservative Party under Stephen Harper. How the party treats people, in the end, is of little consequence when compared to the party's need to stay in power and exercise that power. I lamented earlier about the way the Harper government treats people, how the Conservatives seek to destroy or besmirch the reputations of anyone who criticizes them or simply thinks differently, how they lash out at people who are simply pointing out that the party might have gotten it wrong. From the way the Conservatives attack their critics to the visible contempt in which they hold the press, who are only trying to keep the public informed, it is difficult to see how this party embodies the best ideas of democracy.

It is impossible to predict what will happen in the fall of 2015. It should be apparent, however, that the Conservatives will fight to keep their majority government using any means necessary.

Bibliography

Chapter 1: Chuck Cadman Affair

O'Neil, Peter, "Constituents have convinced him to oppose Liberals, Cadman says," *National Post*, April 26, 2005, 5.

Naumetz, Tim, "Independents may scuttle Harper's plan: Wooed by Liberals," April 28, 2005, 8.

Woods, Allan, and Mike Blanchfield, "Grits called home: Martin orders ministers back from VE day events, other overseas trips," *National Post*, May 3, 2005, 1.

Woods, Allan, and Mike Blanchfield, "Tories ready to go: Harper exits caucus meeting ready to take down Liberals at first opportunity," *National Post*, May 3, 2005, 1.

Kennedy, Mark, "Word at home for Independents is vote for budget, if you want to," *National Post*, May 6, 2005, 6.

Naumetz, Tim, "Tories might delay vote on Liberals' fate: Changing tactics: Poll shows Grits rebounding in Ontario, *National Post*, May 7, 2005, 6.

Robertson, Grant, "Labrador race against time: Liberals want to break tie," *National Post*, May 7, 2005, 8.

Woods, Allan, "Showdown tonight: Tory motion looms, but Grits say it's not confidence matter," *National Post*, May 10, 2005, 1.

Dawson, Anne, and Allan Woods, "Tories win vote, Grits ignore it: Yes: 153 No:150," *National Post*, May 11, 2005, 1.

Dawson, Anne, and Tim Naumetz, "Tories, Bloc shut House in protest," *National Post*, May 12, 2005, 1.

Woods, Allan, "Liberals' fate hinges on independents: Needed to achieve tie vote," *National Post*, May 12, 2005, 4.

Woods, Allan, "Harper agrees top wait for Thursday vote: Shuts down House of Commons for second day," *National Post*, May 14, 2005, 7.

Woods, Allan, and Grant Robertson, "Nfld. Tories waver: MPs fear uproar if Atlantic deal dies with government," *National Post*, May 17, 2005, 1.

Dawson, Anne, "Blonde bombshell: Defection gives Grits vote edge," *National Post*, May 18, 2005, 1.

Ivison, John, "Spring nuptials in a heartless machine," *National Post*, May 18, 2005, 2.

BIBLIOGRAPHY

Woods, Allan, "Stronach takes Conservative secrets to the other side: 'There's a fair amount of stuff she would have been privy to,'" *National Post*, May 18, 2005, 6.

Dawson, Anne, and Allan Woods, "Drama on the hill: Day of political life and death," *National Post*, May 19, 2005, 1.

O'Neill, Peter, "Poll tells Cadman to delay election: 'I've always said I'll do what constituents say,'" *National Post*, May 19, 2005, 7.

Dawson, Anne, Allan Woods, and Grant Robertson, "Grits buy time: Election avoided as Speaker casts the tiebreaker," *National Post*, May 20, 2005, 1.

Greenaway, Norma, and Tim Naumetz, "Liberals skating 'on thin ice' for a while yet: Next vote May 31," *National Post*, May 20, 2005, 4.

Robertson, Grant, "MPs Standing ovation for Cadman," *National Post*, May 20, 2005, 6.

Badelt, Brad, "Victims' rights on agenda, Colter tells Cadman: After confidence vote: 'There was nothing asked for and nothing offered,'" *National Post*, May 24, 2005, 5.

Dawson, Anne, Allan Woods, and Grant Robertson, "Liberals likely to survive non-confidence votes: Conservatives not as eager to force election," *National Post*, June 15, 2005, 6.

"MP Cadman dies at 57," *National Post*, July 11, 2005, 4.

O'Conner, Elaine, "Martin, Harper join hundreds in saying goodbye to Cadman," *National Post*, July 18, 2005, 4.

Schmitz, Cristin, "MPs pay tribute to Chuck Cadman: 'Chuck was an island of dignified calm,'" *National Post*, September 29, 2005, 8.

Martin, Don, "My pick for year's best politician: Cadman stopped an election on his voters' command," *National Post*, December 27, 2005, 5.

"Harper vows to get tough with street-racing plague," *National Post*, May 26, 2006, 6.

"Dying MP offered $1M to topple grits: book; Cadman rejected life insurance deal, author says," *National Post*, February 28, 2008, 5.

Coutts, Matthew, "Policy not possible, experts say," *National Post*, February 29, 2008, 5.

O'Neill, Juliet, and Norma Greenaway, "MPs demand probes of alleged offer; Harper denies dying MP offered insurance policy for aiding Tories," February 29, 2008, 5.

Martin, Don, "Only certainty: Cadman's integrity," *National Post*, February 29, 2008, 6.

O'Neill, Juliet and Greenaway, Norma, "Daughter of Cadman backs mother's claim; Alleged Bribe; MP kept quiet to avoid 'circus' at death, she says," *National Post*, March 1, 2008, 6.

Kay, Jonathan, "Forget who said what: The Cadman scandal is bogus; The idea that a man like Tom Flanagan would risk jail for such a stunt is nonsense," *National Post*, March 1, 2008, 22.

Martin, Don, "Time for an answer, Mr. Harper; PM is the one inflicting damage to his reputation," *National Post*, March 4, 2008, 4.

Hanes, Allison, "PM knew nothing, Cadman's wife says; 'Telling the Truth,'" March 4, 2008, 4.

O'Neill, Juliet, and Norma Greenaway, "Date Deleted From Cadman Book; Publisher yanks May 17 meeting reference," *National Post*, March 5, 2008, 4.

O'Neill, Juliet, and Norma Greenaway, "Tories answer 'simply not credible'; Harper refuses to define 'financial considerations,'" *National Post*, March 6, 2008, 4.

O'Neill, Juliet, "Liberals, Bloc want Cadman hearings; Commons committee would look into bribery charge," *National Post*, March 7, 2008, 4.

O'Neill, Juliet, and Norma Greenaway, "Nearly a third say PM lying: poll," *National Post*, March 8, 2008, 5.

Martin, Don, "Jittery Tory MPs feeling from a ghost," *National Post*, March 13, 2008, 4.

O'Neill, Juliet, "Harper sues Liberal party for $2.5M; Cadman affair," *National Post*, March 14, 2008, 4.

"Justice committee chair walks out again," *National Post*, April 2, 2008, 6.

O'Neill, Juliet, "PM waging 'attack' on public debate: Liberals; Cadman Affair; Party wants jury trial for $2.5M libel suit," *National Post*, May 14, 2008, 4.

Greenaway, Norma, "No criminal charges in Cadman affair, Mounties say," *National Post*, May 17, 2008, 6.

Mayeda, Andrew, "Cadman tape doctored, Tories say; Conservatives file injunction to restrain Liberals from using audio," *National Post*, June 5, 2008, 4.

"Liberals dismiss Prime Minister's $1-million lawsuit as 'outrageous,'" *National Post*, July 5, 2008, 7.

O'Neill, Juliet, "'Author's claim false,'" Cadman's widow says," *National Post*, July 8, 2008, 6.

O'Neill, Juliet, "Cadman biographer stands by recording; Harper Suing Liberals," *National Post*, July 12, 2008, 10.

O'Neill, Juliet, "Audio expert backtracks on Cadman tape," *National Post*, July 15, 2008, 6.

"Judge orders tape with Harper interview on Cadman to be analyzed," *National Post*, July 26, 2008, 6.

Colley, Ted, "Cadman tape not doctored, PM's audio expert says; Alleged Bribe Attempt," *National Post*, October 11, 2008, 15.

O'Neill, Juliet, "Harper's lawyer withdraws from defamation case; Cadman Affair," *National Post*, November 18, 2008, 6.

Mayeda, Andrew, "Harper and Liberal party 'settle all issues' in defamation suit," *National Post*, February 7, 2009, 5.

Chapter 2: In-and-Out Scandal

Dawson, Anna, "Conservatives top election spending at $17.3-million," *National Post*, February 7, 2005, 8.

McGregor, Glen, and Tim Naumetz, "67 candidates involved in Tory ad program: Elections Canada; 'In-And-Out' Process," *National Post*, August 25, 2007, 4.

McGregor, Glen, and Tim Naumetz, "Grits slam Tory ad 'Laundromat'; 2006 Election Spending," *National Post*, September 6, 2007, 4.

McGregor, Glen, "Big spenders do not always win at ballot box; Election spending; Politicians cannot bank on turning a buck into a vote," September 24, 2007, 7.

Akins, David, "Tories' Ads Raised Doubts: Seized files suggest executive uncertain of rules," *National Post*, April 22, 2008, 1.

Smyth, Julie, "Tories made for the exits; 'Too Clever By Half'; Party's secret media briefing ends in farce," *National Post*, April 22, 2008, 4.

"Conservatives knew the rules," *National Post*, April 22, 2008, 14.

Rabson, Mia, "Election Chief accused of bias against Tories; Commons panel looks into alleged spending law violations," *National Post*, July 16, 2008, 8.

McGregor, Glen, "Conservatives fail to appear before financing probe; Elections Advertising," *National Post*, August 14, 2008, 6.

McGregor, Glen, "Raid on Ottawa HQ included 'overbroad' seizure: Tories," *National Post*, January 23, 2009, 6.

McGregor, Glen, "Tories drop 'in and out' money strategy," *National Post*, March 9, 2009, 4.

McGregor, Glen, "Tories win court case on election ad spending; 'In-And-Out'; Elections Canada ordered to accept candidate claims," *National Post*, July 29, 2010, 7.

Kennedy, Mark, "Tories charged over election spending; Allegedly overspent through 'in-and-out' advertising in 2006," *National Post*, February 25, 2011, 7.

McGregor, Glen, "Tory party official charged in scandal has new job with Auditor-General; 'Not on audits,'" *National Post*, March 3, 2011, 4.

"The Ins and Outs," *National Post* March 3, 2011, 4.

"Tories drop appeal over vote spending; 'Plays by same rules,'" March 7, 2011, 4.

"Only 4 in 10 know about 'in-out scheme': poll," *National Post*, March 17, 2011, 11.

Chapter 3: Afghan Detainee Scandal

Blanchfield, Mike, "Military probes Afghan prisoner abuse charges," *National Post*, February 7, 2007, 6.

Blanchfield, Mike, "No room for two inquiries," *National Post*, February 10, 2007, 6.

"Military police commission chief opens broader abuse investigation," *National Post*, February 27, 2007, 8.

Thomson, Graham, "O'Connor defuses controversy over detainee comments," *National Post*, March 12, 2007, 6.

Thomson, Graham, "O'Connor meets Afghan human rights watchdog," *National Post*, March 15, 2007, 8.

Fitzpatrick, Meagan, "O'Connor admits prisoners error: Refuses to resign," *National Post*, March 20, 2007, 8.

"Harper accuses Liberals of showing 'passion' for Taliban, not supporting troops," *National Post*, March 22, 2007, 5.

Blanchfield, Mike, "Ignatieff seeks Tory apology times two," *National Post*, March 23, 2007, 4.

O'Neill, Juliet, "PM rejects Taliban transfers; Liberals suggest moving prisoners to Canada," *National Post*, April 24, 2007, 4.

Dougherty, Kevin, "Taliban 'torturers' not wanted here; Day," *National Post*, April 25, 2007, 1.

Blanchfield, Mike, and Juliet O'Neill, "Detainee policy news to Tory MPs," *National Post*, April 26, 2007, 1.

Blanchfield, Mike, "Afghan detainee agreement still being negotiated: aide," *National Post*, April 27, 2007, 6.

Ivison, John, "Torture allegations are lies, Afghan official says," *National Post*, April 28, 2007. 5.

Mayeda, Andrew, and Mike Blanchfield, "Martin approved a detainee policy," *National Post*, May 3, 2007, 6.

Mayeda, Andrew, and Mike Blanchfield, "Military says detainee was beaten by Afghans," *National Post*, May 4, 2007, 1.

O'Neill, Juliet, "Afghan detainees make torture claims," *National Post*, June 7, 2007, 8.

O'Neill, Juliet, "Defence Boss Busted Down to Revenue," *National Post*, August 15, 2007, 4.

Foot, Richard, "Military loses battle over Afghan policy," *National Post*, November 6, 2007, 8.

Goodspeed, Peter, "Torture widespread in Afghanistan, Amnesty says," *National Post*, November 13, 2007, 18.

Blanchfield, Mike, "Afghan detainee transfers suspended in November; House not told," *National Post*, January 24, 2008, 1.

Blanchfield, Mike, "Detainee secret necessary: lawyer," *National Post*, January 25, 2008, 4.

Blanchfield, Mike, "Dion knew about detainees, he admits; Sworn to secrecy," *National Post*, January 26, 2008, 1.

"Afghan prisoners are held at Canadian Forces base in Kandahar, CBC reports," *National Post*, February 1, 2008, 6.

Blanchfield, Mike, "Federal court cites concerns over detainee transfers," *National Post*, February 8, 2008, 4.

"Charter can't protect Afghans; Detainee ruling," *National Post*, March 13, 2008, 1.

Naumetz, Tim, "Ombudsman admits aiding DND secrecy," *National Post*, May 28, 2008, 9.

Mayeda, Amanda, "Afghan detainees' treatment probed; December hearings," *National Post*, October 1, 2008, 8.

Baer, Nicole, "No evidence detainees mistreated, military police say," *National Post*, October 4, 2008, 7.

Tibbetts, Janice, " Ottawa warned about detainees; former envoy," *National Post*, October 15, 2009, 4.

Tibbetts, Janice, "Tory defence minister pleads ignorance on Afghan torture," *National Post*, October 16, 2009, 5.

Martin, Don, "Hillier refuses to stay silent," *National Post*, October 20, 2009, 1.

Tibbetts, Janice, "Canada ignored torture: Ex-envoy," *National Post*, November 19, 2009, 1.

Tibbetts, Janice, "Minister calls abuse allegations hearsay," *National Post*, November 20, 2009, 1.

Akin, David, "Transfers halted three times this year: DND," *National Post*, November 24, 2009, 4.

Akin, David, "PM stands by soldiers in torture hearing," *National Post*, November 25, 2009, 4.

Tibbets, Janice, and David Akin, "No mention of torture, generals say," *National Post*, November 26, 2009, 4.

Tibbets, Janice, and David Akin, "Torture cover-up not true," *National Post*, November 27, 2009, 1.

Alcoba, Natalie, "Portrait of an envoy," *National Post*, November 28, 2009, 14.

Fisher, Matthew, "Red Cross official critical of diplomat," *National Post*, November 30, 2009, 9.

O'Neill, Juliet, and Janice Tibbetts, "'No one turned a blind eye'; Abuse allegations not ignored, ministers insist," *National Post*, December 10, 2009, 4.

O'Neill, Juliet, "Government won't open detainee files," *National Post*, December 12, 2009, 15.

Cross, Allison, "Off until after Olympics Legislation dies; GG prorogues Parliament at PM's request," *National Post*, December 31, 2009, 4.

O'Neill, Juliet, "Rules will stop detainee abuse, NATO chief says," *National Post*, January 14, 2010, 11.

O'Neill, Juliet, "Way cleared for more detainee hearings," *National Post*, January 28, 2010, 4.

Blackwell, Tom, "Ottawa asks judge to review release of detainee documents," National Post, March 6, 2010, 9.

O'Neill, Juliet, "Canada mum of Afghan detainees," *National Post*, April 14, 2010, 6.

Duffy, Andrew, "Afghans told to take on detainees, court told," *National Post*, April 20, 2010, 5.

O'Neill, Juliet, "Ruling may lead to election," *National Post*, April 26, 2010, 4.

O'Neill, Juliet, and David Akin, "PM loses detainee file fight," *National Post*, April 28, 2010, 1.

Kennedy, Mark, and Althia Raj, "Detainees were likely abused: Dion," *National Post* June 23, 2011, 4.

Chapter 4: Maxime Bernier Affair

Cormier, Ryan, "Minister backs off criticism," *National Post*, April 15, 2008, 4.

"Move over MacKay: Bernier claims 'sexiest man in the house' title," *National Post*, May 1, 2008, 10.

Blanchfield, Mike, "Harper condemns opposition as 'old busybodies,'" *National Post*, May 9, 2008, 6.

Martin, Don, "Bumbling Bernier quits," *National Post*, May 27, 2008, 1.

Blanchfield, Mike, "Tories' failed hope in Quebec," *National Post*, May 27, 2008, 6.

Blanchfield, Mike, and David Akin, "Bernier probe demanded," *National Post*, May 28, 2008, 1.

Cowan, James, "Do cument rules fuzz, experts say," *National Post*, May 28, 2008. 4.

Mayeda, Andrew, "Experts list possible bedroom spies," *National Post*, May 28, 2008, 4.

"Timeline," *National Post*, May 28, 2008, 4.

Leong, Melissa, "If she had just worn a pantsuit," *National Post*, May 28, 2008, 5.

Martin, Don, "Latest theory, Bernier set up," *National Post*, May 29, 2008, 1.

Blanchfield, Mike, "Liberals hint spy agency consulted," *National Post*, May 29, 2008, 4.

Akin, David, "'Sexy' scandal front page greets PM in Italy," *National Post*, May 29, 2008, 4.

Hamilton, Graeme, "Bernier used me, ex-lover alleges," *National Post*, May 30, 2008, 4.

Blanchfield, Mike, "Canadians divided over Bernier affair: Poll," *National Post*, May 31, 2008, 4.

Akin, David, "Couillard linked to Mafioso," *National Post*, June 4, 2008, 6.

Ivison, John, "Couillard not our department: RCMP," *National Post*, June 11, 2008, 4.

Thompson, Elizabeth, "Senior advisor who once dated Couillard resigns," *National Post*, June 12, 2008, 7.

Thompson, Elizabeth, "Couillard did not use me: ex-boyfriend," *National Post*, June 13, 2008, 4.

Thompson, Elizabeth, "Couillard refuses to testify before MPs committee," *National Post*, June 17, 2008, 4.

"Former girlfriend of toppled minister to write autobiography," *National Post*, June 21, 2008, 13.

Hamilton, Graeme, "Forces' e-mails track 'Jos. Louis Diplomacy,'" *National Post*, June 26, 2008, 4.

"Not aware of ex-girlfriend's past: Bernier," *National Post*, June 26, 2008, 4.

"Bernier did not cause 'significant injury' to national interests, review concludes," *National Post*, August 2, 2008, 4.

Martin, Don, "Reports' timing a trashy move," *National Post*, August 6, 2008, 1.

"Calls grow for new Bernier investigation," *National Post*, August 7, 2008, 6.

Offman, Craig, "Couillard defends tell-all memoir," *National Post*, October 2, 2008, 1.

Ivison, John, "Toss classified papers, Bernier told ex-lover," *National Post*, October 2, 2008, 6.

Couillard, Julie, "The love of her life," *National Post*, October 4, 2008, 23.

Couillard, Julie, "Memories of Maxime," *National Post*, October 6, 2008, 14.

Couillard, Julie, "'Could you put this in the garbage for me?'" *National Post*, October 7, 2008, 19.

"Dress that put Couillard in media crosshair back in the news," *National Post*, April 30, 2009, 5.

Ivison, John, "Bernier eyes 'more prudent' second act," *National Post*, May 26, 2009, 6.

Greenaway, Norma, "Bernier's forgotten papers finally released," *National Post*, September 4, 2009, 7.

Chapter 5: 2008 Prorogue of Parliament

Martin, Don, "Grim talk for grim times; Economic crisis dominates Throne Speech," *National Post*, November 20, 2008, 1.

Vieira, Paul, "Flaherty says more cash may follow $33B boost," *National Post*, November 21, 2008, 5.

Vieira, Paul, "Deficit could hit $14B, warns budget officer," *National Post*, November 21, 2008, 6.

Martin, Don, "Tories to trim pay, perks," *National Post*, November 26, 2008, 1.

Ivison, John, "Tories seek to kill party subsidies," *National Post*, November 27, 2008, 1.

Vieira, Paul, "Budget to be presented on Jan. 27," *National Post*, December 1, 2008, 1.

Vieira, Paul, "Drama on the Hill: Opposition determined to form coalition," *National Post*, December 1, 2008, 1.

Vieira, Paul, "Coalition would push 2-year stimulus plan," *National Post*, December 2, 2008, 7.

Akin, David, De Souza, Mike, Mayeda, Andrew and O'Neill, Juliet, "Harper pleads for more time as Liberals seek to lead coalition government for next 30 months," *National Post*, December 2, 2008, 1.

Ivison, John, "Harper will go down swinging; Like to request Parliament be prorogued," *National Post*, December 3, 2008, 1.

Akin, David, Andrew Mayeda, and Juliet O'Neill, "Harper Vows a Fight; PM to visit Governor-General today," *National Post*, December 4, 2008, 1.

Vieira, Paul, "More stimulus in budget: Flaherty," *National Post*, December 4, 2008, 10.

Akin, David, "Harper wins reprieve until Jan. 26, pledges to try to build trust," *National Post*, December 5, 2008, 1.

Vieira, Paul, "'Government have to eat crow on budget,'" *Financial Post*, December 5, 2008, 10.

O'Neill, Juliet, "Dion to quit as Liberals mull new leader; May resign today," *National Post*, December 8, 2008, 1.

Martin, Don, "Rae Bows Out For Ignatieff," National Post, December 10, 2008, 1.

O'Toole, Megan, "Harper finds olive branch; January Budget," *National Post*, December 10, 2008, 6.

Ivison, John, "Ignatieff backs away from cliff," *National Post*, December 11, 2008, 1.

Akin, David, "Tories To Fill Senate; Senators to be appointed before coalition gets chance," *National Post*, December 11, 2008, 1.

Tibbetts, Janice, "Ignatieff, Harper hold talks," *National Post*, December 13, 2008, 4.

Vieira, Paul, "Ottawa faces up to reality of deficits," *Financial Post*, December 19, 2008, 1.

Asper, David, "Unchartered Waters; We made it this time. But could Canadian democracy survive another constitutional crisis?" *National Post*, January 2, 2009, 14.

Akin, David, "Tories earmark $1B for job creation; More details on budget expected today," *National Post*, January 26, 2009, 4.

O'Neill, Juliet, and Andrew Mayeda, "Liberals put PM on 'probation'; Coalition dead as Ignatieff accused of propping up Harper," *National Post*, January 29, 2009, 1.

O'Neill, Juliet, and Andrew Mayeda, "Liberals back Tory budget; Rebellion defused," *National Post*, February 4, 2009, 4.

Chapter 6: F-35 Purchase Scandal

Stone, Laura, "65 new jets needed to 'meet threats,' MacKay says," *National Post*, July 17, 2010, 4.

McDowell, Adam, "Will one engine be enough?" *National Post*, July 17, 2010, 4.

"Liberals seek probe into jet contract," *National Post*, July 22, 2010, 6.

Pugliese, David, "DND computers used to delete criticism," *National Post*, July 29, 2010, 7.

Ivison, John, "'Sole-sourcing stupid:' DND buzz on jets," *National Post*, September 14, 2010, 6.

"F-35 plan good for future deals: Ambrose," *National Post*, September 15, 2010, 6.

"Mission Control; F-35 Jet Hearings," *National Post*, September 16, 2010, 4.

MacKay, Peter, "65 F-35s: Why there were sole-sourced..." *National Post*, September 16, 2010, 15.

Pugliese, David, "Jet competition meant to start this year: report," *National Post*, September 20, 2010, 5.

McDowell, Adam, "Turbulence dogs F-35 stealth fighter plane," *National Post*, October 7, 2010, 4.

BIBLIOGRAPHY

Ivison, John, "Helicopter deal plays spoiler," *National Post*, October 27, 2010, 1.

Fitzpatrick, Meagan, "Liberals would cancel F-35 jet deal, Ignatieff says," *National Post*, October 28, 2010, 4.

Cohen, Tobi, "Canadian fighter-jet purchase vital: Gates," *National Post*, January 28, 2011, 5.

"Proposed F-35 fighter jets would not have capability to refuel mid-air," January 31, 2011, 8.

Pugliese, David, "Tory MP knocks stealth-jet critics," *National Post*, March 7, 2011, 4.

Cohen, Tobi, and Adam McDowell, "F-35 fighters could cost billions extra, report says," *National Post*, March 11, 2011, 4.

McDowell, Adam, "Liberals play politics with F-35 jet promise," *National Post*, March 29, 2011, 5.

"F-35 fighter jets to cost $100M each, US Accountability Office says," *National Post*, March 31, 2011, 5.

Pugliese, David, "F-35 fighter jet's cost to top $75M, defence says," *National Post*, April 27, 2011, 8.

Den Tandt, Michael, "F-35 purchase 'a real mess,'" *National Post*, October 28, 2011, 4.

Berthiaume, Lee, "Two-year delay on F-35s not a concern: Tories," *National Post*, November 9, 2011, 5.

Berthiaume, Lee, "Cracks found in jet fighters' airframe, Pentagon says," *National Post*, December 3, 2011, 4.

"Canada's next fighter jet?" *National Post*, December 31, 2011, 8.

Ivison, John, "Ottawa sets sights on armed drones," *National Post*, February 15, 2012, 1.

"Tories' F-35 plans hit turbulence," *National Post*, March 14, 2012, 5.

Ivison, John, "Auditor to slam F-35 jet process," *National Post*, March 16, 2012, 1.

Berthiaume, Lee, "DND glossed over F-35 warnings: documents," *National Post*, March 17, 2012, 4.

Davis, Jeff, "DND met repeatedly with Lockheed on F-35s," *National Post*, March 27, 2012, 6.

Ivison, John, "Tories to reopen F-35 debate," *National Post*, April 3, 2012, 1.

Ivison, John, "Flack for PM, bombs for DND," *National Post*, April 4, 2012, 1.

Coyne, Andrew, "MacKay's defence of F-35 estimates doesn't add up," *National Post*, April 10, 2012, 4.

Berthiaume, Lee, "MacKay 'not too bright?' Liberal MP wonders," *National Post*, April 12, 2012, 4.

"Questions & Answers; Flight of the F-35 Joint Strike Fighter," *National Post*, April 23, 2012, 6.

Ivison, John, "Air Force stands by its choice," *National Post*, May 2, 2012, 9.

Berthiaume, Lee, "Full costs of jet withheld: budget officer," *National Post*, May 4, 2012, 4.

Berthiaume, Lee, "F-35 may still be on the table: Lockheed," *National Post*, May 25, 2012, 6.

"Panellists appointed to oversee F-35 case," *National Post*, June 14, 2012, 5.

"KPMG to assess F-35 fighter program costs," *National Post*, September 8, 2012, 7.

"Let loose Avro Arrow, company urges Tories," *National Post*, September 10, 2012, 3.

Shimooka, Richard, "The evolution of an F-35," *National Post*, November 2, 2012, 14.

Ivison, John, "F-35 plans losing altitude," *National Post*, November 30, 2012, 1.

"Canada's next fighter jet?" *National Post*, December 1, 2012, 10.

Den Tandt, Michael, "F-35 dead in the air," *National Post*, December 7, 2012, 1.

Ivison, John, "Despite all rumours, the F-35 is alive," *National Post*, December 8, 2012, 2.

Tomesco, Frederic, "Canada solicits companies for jet data," *National Post*, March 4, 2013, 4.

Berthiaume, Lee, "Pentagon report blasts F-35s for testing issues," *National Post*, March 7, 2013, 10.

Berthiaume, Lee, "Ottawa was ready to lose fighter jets," *National Post*, April 29, 2013, 5.

Deveau, Scott, "Dassault urges open contest for fighters," *Financial Post*, June 20, 2013, 4.

Berthiaume, Lee, "Countdown on F-35 decision begins," *National Post*, April 14, 2014, 4.

"Costs to operate F-35s could double, report says," *National Post*, April 30, 2014, 8.

"Panel to deliver report on F-35 alternatives," *National Post*, June 12, 2014, 9.

Berthiaume, Lee, "Tories refuse to release 'public' F-35 report," *National Post*, June 12, 2014, 9.

Pugliese, David, "Jet fighter review over to Tories," *National Post*, June 13, 2014, 11.

"Fighter jet timeline," *National Post*, June 13, 2014, 4.

Chapter 7: Guergis-Jaffer Affair

"Guergis apologizes to airport staff," *National Post*, February 26, 2010, 6.

Nguyen, Linda, "Ex-MP gets 'a break,' judge says," *National Post*, March 10, 2010, 4.

Brean, Joseph, "Jaffer plea deal 'not so unusual': lawyer," *National Post*, March 13, 2010, 12.

"Tories on defensive over airport incident," *National Post*, March 20, 2010, 12.

Martin, Don, "Guergis wobbly after new misstep," *National Post*, March 31, 2010, 6.

Martin, Don, "Fall from role model to rubble," *National Post*, April 9, 2010, 4.

Akin, David, "Guergis faces heat over ex-MP husband," *National Post*, April 9, 2010, 4.

Martin, Don, "Guergis too toxic for Tories to defend," *National Post*, April 10, 2010, 1.

Akin, David, and Norma Greenaway, "Allegations are 'baseless,' Guergis says," *National Post*, April 10, 2010, 6.

Akin, David, "PM acted on 'third-party' allegations," *National Post*, April 13, 2010, 4.

Akin, David, "Guergis probe put on hold: ethics chief," *National Post*, April 14, 2010, 4.

Kari, Shannon, "Private eye under siege," *National Post*, April 16. 2010, 1.

McParland, Kelly, "The case against Helena Guergis," *National Post*, April 16, 2010, 14.

De Souza, Mike, "Guergis denies links to Green Business," *National Post*, April 17, 2010, 6.

Martin, Don, "Jaffer's lack of remorse hits home," *National Post*, April 17, 2010, 6.

Akin, David, "Jaffer will face Commons committee," *National Post*, April 20, 2010, 4.

Akin, David, "Guergis asks to delay her appearance," *National Post*, April 21, 2010, 6.

Kari, Shannon, "Jaffer's Commons' probe begins today," *National Post*, April 21, 2010, 6.

Akin, David, "Jaffer denies allegations," *National Post*, April 22, 2010, 1.

Martin, Don, "Somehow, things just got worse," *National Post*, April 22, 2010, 8.

Nguyen, Linda, "Businessman eager to tell 'his side of the story,'" *National Post*, April 22, 2010, 8.

Akin, David, "Jaffer's partner blames racism," *National Post*, April 23, 2010, 1.

Akin, David, "Jaffer sought $135m: documents," *National Post*, April 23, 2010, 4.

"Jaffer used wife's office for business," *National Post*, April 27, 2010, 6.

Akin, David, "Do cuments show Jaffer used wife's resources," *National Post*, April 29, 2010, 1.

Akin, David, "Jaffer was 'money access point,'" *National Post*, April 29, 2010, 4.

Akin, David, "Jaffer access breached federal rules: Liberals," *National Post*, May 4, 2010, 5.

Akin, David, "Guergis decries decision to strip her of her nominations," *National Post*, May 7, 2010, 4.

Laidlaw, Katherine, "PM didn't tell me what I had done: Guergis," *National Post*, May 11, 2010, 1.

Laidlaw, Katherine, "'I'm hurt by the Prime Minister': Guergis," *National Post*, May 11, 2010, 1.

Laidlaw, Katherine, "Guergis told of allegations, PMO says," *National Post*, May 12, 2010, 6.

Akin, David, "Investigator 'unwilling participant,'" *National Post*, May 13, 2010, 4.

Stinson, Scott, "A roller-coaster ride," *National Post*, May 14, 2010, 4.

"Ethics commissioner fines Guergis $100 for failing to report mortgage," *National Post*, May 21, 2010, 8.

"Guergis to PM: come clean on allegations," *National Post*, June 4, 2010, 6.

"Unspecified health concerns will keep Guergis from House committee," *National Post*, June 8, 2010, 8.

"MP angry at Jaffer's committee snub," *National Post*, June 9, 2010, 6.

Akin, David, "Guergis fired over alleged fraud scheme," *National Post*, June 10, 2010, 1.

Fitzpatrick, Meagan, "Jaffer misses hearing to be with wife at doctor's," *National Post*, June 17, 2010, 4.

Fitzpatrick, Meagan, "Jaffer attacks former colleagues' treatment of wife," *National Post*, June 18, 2010, 8.

Fitzpatrick, Meagan, "RCMP clear Guergis and Jaffer," *National Post*, July 22, 2010, 6.

Fitzpatrick, Meagan, and Linda Nguyen, "Guergis demands meeting with Harper," *National Post*, July 23, 2010, 4.

Vallis, Mary, "Guergis recovering after car accident," *National Post*, August 13, 2010, 8.

"Guergis gives birth to healthy boy named Zavier Rahim Nizarali," *National Post*, December 16, 2010, 8.

"'There was a time I would do anything Mr. Harper asked of me,'" *National Post*, March 26, 2011, 7.

Carlson, Kathryn Blaze, "'Concerted effort to perpetrate lies,'" *National Post*, April 16, 2011, 4.

Minsky, Amy, "Guergis broke code of ethics: watchdog," *National Post*, July 15, 2011, 4.

Kennedy, Mark, and Lee Berthiaume, "Guergis sues Harper, Tory party," *National Post*, December 23, 2011, 4.

Chapter 8: Robocalls Scandal

McGregor, Glen, and Stephen Maher, "Fake election calls traced to firm with Tory links," *National Post*, February 23, 2012, 1.

McGregor, Glen, and Stephen Maher, "Calls not linked to us: Harper," *National Post*, February 24, 2011, 4.

McGregor, Glen, and Stephen Maher, "Voters received fake live calls," *National Post*, February 25, 2012, 4.

Stechyson, Natalie, "34 ridings affected by crank calls to voters," *National Post*, February 27, 2011, 6.

Press, Jordan, and Lee Berthiaume, "Harper dismisses allegations of wrongdoing," *National Post*, February 28, 2012, 4.

McGregor, Glen, and Stephen Maher, "Cell traced to 'Pierre Poutine,'" *National Post*, February 29, 2012, 4.

"Ridings allegedly targeted by Robocalls," *National Post*, February 29, 2012, 4.

Stechyson, Natalie, "Campaign chair denies Tories behind robocalls," *National Post*, March 5, 2012, 4.

Cross, Allison, "Elections list full of errors," *National Post*, March 6, 2012, 4.

Ivison, John, "Robocalls answer in Tory servers," *National Post*, March 6, 2012, 4.

Ivison, John, "Closing in on Pierre Poutine," *National Post*, March 9, 2012, 1.

Kennedy, Mark, "Hold new votes in robocall riding: poll," *National Post*, March 10, 2012, 5.

Ivison, John, "Robocalls sent across Ontario," *National Post*, March 17, 2012, 4.

McGregor, Glen, and Stephen Maher, "'No idea of calls' origins': candidate," *National Post*, March 20, 2012, 5.

McGregor, Glen, and Stephen Maher, "Robocalls 'absolutely outrageous,'" *National Post*, March 30, 2012, 4.

McGregor, Glen, and Stephen Maher, "Robocalls sent from Tory IP address: investigators," *National Post*, May 5, 2012, 11.

"Court Oks attempt to overturn results," *National Post*, July 20, 2012, 4.

McGregor, Glen, and Stephen Maher, "Liberal MP fined by CRTC for Guelph robocall," *National Post*, August 25, 2012, 11.

"Former Tory staffer says he's 'not going to take the fall' for robocall scandal," *National Post*, November 1, 2012, 5.

McGregor, Glen, and Stephen Maher, "Voters thought robocalls were 'scam,'" *National Post*, November 17, 2012, 12.

McGregor, Glen, and Stephen Maher, "'Deceptive' robocalls followed the rules: Harper," *National Post*, February 7, 2013, 6.

Maher, Stephen, and Glen McGregor, "Tory staffer charged in robocall probe," *National Post*, April 3, 2013, 5.

Maher, Stephen, "Telemarketer, parties fined over robocalls," *National Post*, May 30, 2013, 4.

McGregor, Glen, "Names of robocalls witnesses released," *National Post*, November 16, 2013, 4.

Maher, Stephen, "Tory staffer testifies in robocalls case," *National Post*, April 4, 2014, 4.

Maher, Stephen, "Trial may reveal ID of 'poutine,'" *National Post*, June 2, 2014, 4.

McGregor, Glen, and Stephen Maher, "Robocall plan not embraced: witnesses," *National Post*, June 3, 2014, 1.

Maher, Stephen, "Showdown looms at Robocalls trial," *National Post*, June 4, 2014, 4.

Maher, Stephen, and Glen McGregor, "Testimony appears to link Sona to calls," *National Post*, June 5, 2014, 5.

Maher, Stephen, "Robocall remarks recounted," *National Post*, June 6, 2014, 6.

Maher, Stephen, "Robocalls scandal a team effort, court told," *National Post*, June 10, 2014, 7.

Chapter 9: Omnibus Bills

"Harper's new omnibus budget bill a stealth blow to civil servants," *Toronto Star*, Oct. 23, 2013.

"Feds on collision course with courts over omnibus crime law," Retrieved Oct. 1, 2014, from www.cbc.ca.

"Harper government omnibus crime bill: Canadian justice gets a major makeover," Retrieved Oct. 1. 2014, from www.huffingtonpost.ca.

Ivison, John, "How Stephen Harper learned to love the omnibus bill," Retrieved Oct. 1, 2014, from www.nationalpost.ca.

"What worries critics about omnibus crime bill," Retrieved Oct. 1, 2014, from www.cbc.ca.

Galloway, Gloria and Seguin, Rheal, "Harper's promise fulfilled as House passes crime bill," Retrieved Oct. 1, 2014, from www.theglobeandmail.com.

McGregor, Janyce, "22 changes in the budget bill fine print," Retrieved Oct. 1, 2014, from www.cbc.ca.

Pedwell, Terry. "Idle No More vs. Bill C-45: First Nations leaders launch national protest in Ottawa as movement grows." Retrieved Oct. 1, 2014, from www.huffingtonpost.ca.

"Nine questions about Idle No More," Retrieved Oct. 1, 2014, from www.cbc.ca.

Selley, Chris, "Harper's relations with First Nations was stifled by omnibus bill," Retrieved Oct. 1, 2014, from www.nationalpost.ca.

Chapter 10: Senate Expense Scandal

"No 'fast-track' for Senator Mike Duffy's health card," *National Post*, February 5, 2013, 6.

"What happened to Brazeau?" *National Post*, February 9, 2013, 7.

Press, Jordan, "Housing scandal puts Senate names on the line," *National Post*, February 12, 2013, 6.

Press, Jordan, "Housing allowance claims rife among Senate," *National Post*, February 14, 2013, 4.

Bryden, Joan, "Duffy to pay back housing allowance," *National Post*, February 23, 2013, 6.

Cheadle, Bruce, "No new issues in housing probe: Senate," *National Post*, March 1, 2013, 4.

"Unclear if Duffy repaid housing money," *National Post*, April 19, 2013.

Press, Jordan, "Duffy repays $90,000 in housing claim money," *National Post*, April 20, 2013, 11.

Bryden, Joan, and Jennifer Ditchburn, "Senate expense furor; Calls for police probe in wake of audit," *National Post*, May 10, 2013, 4.

Woods, Michael, "RCMP probes Senate expenses," *National Post*, May 13, 2013, 4.

Coyne, Andrew, "The Duffy bailout: what were they thinking?" *National Post*, May 16, 2013, 1.

Press, Jordan, and Jason Fekete, "Watchdog looking into $90,000 gift to Duffy," *National Post*, May 16, 2013, 4.

Press, Jordan, and Jennifer Ditchburn, "Duffy quits Tory caucus," *National Post*, May 17, 2013, 1.

Press, Jordan, "Harper sticks by chief of staff," *National Post*, May 17, 2013, 1.

Woods, Michael, and Mark Kennedy, "Wallin quits caucus until audit complete," *National Post*, May 18, 2013, 4.

Ivison, John, "Missed chance for Harper to make right," *National Post*, May 22, 2013, 4.

"Senate committee reopens investigation into Duffy's $90,000 expenses claim," *National Post*, May 22, 2013, 5.

Ditchburn, Jennifer, "Senate committee dropped sections of Duffy report," *National Post*, May 23, 2013, 4.

Press, Jordan, "Duffy demands expense inquiry," *National Post*, May 24, 2013, 4.

BIBLIOGRAPHY 277

Edmiston, Jake, "Only 1 in 10 would keep Senate as is," *National Post*, May 27, 2013, 4.

Press, Jordan, and Michael Woods, "Duffy expenses referred to RCMP," *National Post*, May 29, 2013, 1.

Press, Jordan, and Michael Woods, "Mulcair drills PM on Duffy," *National Post*, May 29, 2013, 4.

"Duffy sought party perks, CBC report indicates," *National Post*, May 31, 2013, 4.

"Duffy approached PM about claims," *National Post*, June 1, 2013, 4.

Press, Jordan, "Liberal senators' tab now $230K," *National Post*, June 13, 2013, 1.

Bryden, Joan, "RCMP to probe Wright-Duffy cheque," *National Post*, June 14, 2013, 4.

Rennie, Steve, and Joan Bryden, "Harb now part of RCMP probe," *National Post*, June 21, 2013, 4.

Smith-Karstens, Gemma, "Group uses Duffy balloon to focus on senate future," *National Post*, July 19, 2013, 4.

Ivison, John, "Walls close in on Wallin," *National Post*, August 13, 2013, 1.

"The Wallin audit: A senate committee overseeing Pamela Wallin's spending audit recommended Tuesday that the RCMP be called in, that she pay back about $82,000 above what she's already repaid for ineligible expenses and that she be grounded from travelling unless the Senate says she can fly," *National Post*, August 14, 2013, 4.

"AG planning to audit all senators," *National Post*, August 16, 2013, 4.

Ivison, John, " The Senate scandals: If Duffy's case reaches court, PM will be called as witness, sources say," *National Post*, August 17, 2013, 1.

Fekete, Jason, "Harper to prorogue Parliament until October," *National Post*, August 20, 2013, 1.

De Souza, Mike, and Tobi Cohen, "Harb quits Senate, repays $231,000," *National Post*, August 27, 2013, 1.

"RCMP interviewing Senators on Wallin," *National Post*, September 27, 2013, 5.

Press, Jordan, "Duffy ally paid for no work, RCMP say," *National Post*, October 9, 2013, 1.

Press, Jordan, "PM's chief aide had Duffy file, RCMP says," *National Post*, October 10, 2013, 6.

Press, Jordan, "Senate moves to suspend pay of three embattled senators," *National Post*, October 18, 2013, 4.

Press, Jordan, "Tories bristle at Senate decision," *National Post*, October 19, 2013, 16.

Ivison, John, "Duffy's lawyer goes on offence," *National Post*, October 22, 2013, 1.

Ivison, John, "Duffy doesn't go quietly, puts PM at the scene," *National Post*, October 23, 2013, 1.

"Senator believed his honesty was on line," *National Post*, October 23, 2013, 5.

"Do what we want or else," *National Post*, October 23, 2013, 5.

Ivison, John, "Wallin targets Tory tactics," *National Post*, October 24, 2013, 1.

Coyne, Andrew, "PM denies Duffy threat," *National Post*, October 24, 2013, 1.

Press, Jordan, and Jason Fekete, "LeBreton contradicts Duffy's version," *National Post*, October 25, 2013, 4.

Edmiston, Jake, and Andrea Hill, "Top Tory Senators shy from motion," *National Post*, October 28, 2013, 1.

"Duffy expands on PMO payments for him," *National Post*, October 29, 2013, 4.

Press, Jordan, and Tobi Cohen, "Softer suspension motion in the works," *National Post*, October 31, 2013, 4.

Bryden, Joan, "Ousters could spread: Brazeau," *National Post*, November 5, 2013, 4.

Ivison, John, "Second thought, but who's on first? Senate suspends trio as business of governing stalls," *National Post*, November 6, 2013, 1.

Bryden, Joan, "Three suspended senators could still qualify for 'gold-plated' pensions," *National Post*, November 7, 2013, 4.

Press, Jordan, "PM's aide broke law, RCMP say," *National Post*, November 21, 2013, 1.

Kennedy, Mark, "PMO denies Harper was in the loop on repayment," *National Post*, November 22, 2013, 4.

Press, Jordan, "Senators may be questioned under oath," *National Post*, January 3, 2014, 4.

Press, Jordan, "Senate audit on travel, expenses forthcoming," *National Post*, January 27, 2014, 4.

Spears, Tom, and Stephen Maher, "Brazeau pleads not guilty to assault charges," *National Post*, April 11, 2014, 7.

Fekete, Jason, and Mark Kennedy, "RCMP clears Wright in Duffy scandal," *National Post*, April 16, 2014, 1.

Press, Jordan, "Wallin regrets repaying in full," *National Post*, April 25, 2014, 10.

Press, Jordan, "RCMP pores over Duffy's hotel bills," *National Post*, June 6, 2014, 7.

Do, Trinh Theresa, "Mike Duffy reached out to Peruvian woman claiming to be daughter," CBC, www.cbc.ca (retrieved July 22).

Press, Jordan and Hurley, Meghan, "Mike Duffy charged Senate for travel expenses to funerals:

RCMP," *Ottawa Citizen,* www.ottawacitizen.com (retrieved July 22).

McGregor, Glen, "Duffy 'looking forward' to getting case quickly to court," *Ottawa Citizen,* www.ottawacitizen.com (retrieved July 22).

Peter Boer

PETER BOER is a bestselling author and has a background in journalism, having served as reporter and co-editor for the *St. Albert Gazette* newspaper. Peter has a degree in psychology from the University of Alberta in Edmonton and a graduate diploma in journalism from Concordia University in Montréal. In his commitment to lifelong learning, he has taken a leap in his career and will now be teaching the finer points of writing to his students. He has 11 other books to his credit, including *Bush Pilots: Canada's Wilderness Daredevils*, *Canadian Spies and Spies in Canada*, *Canadian Crime Investigations: Hunting Down Serial Killers* and *Canadian Security Intelligence Service* for Folklore Publishing.